SINCE
1854

MECHANICS' INSTITUTE

LIBRARY & CHESS ROOM

57 Post Street, San Francisco, CA 94104
(415) 393-0101

MONEY,
BLOOD AND
REVOLUTION

PRAISE FOR

THE ORIGIN OF FINANCIAL CRISES

BY GEORGE COOPER

"A must-read"

THE ECONOMIST

"Awesomely lucid"

DOMINIC LAWSON, THE INDEPENDENT

"Eerily entertaining"

NEWSWEEK

"The most intellectually enriching analysis I have found"

ALISTAIR BLAIR,
INVESTORS CHRONICLE

"A well-written book...Cooper's most novel doctrine is that investors do not have to be irrational to generate bubbles"

FINANCIAL TIMES

"George Cooper framed it so well in his book"

WALL STREET JOURNAL

MONEY, BLOOD AND REVOLUTION

How Darwin and the doctor of King Charles I
could turn economics into a science

GEORGE COOPER

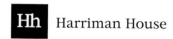 Harriman House

HARRIMAN HOUSE LTD
3A Penns Road
Petersfield
Hampshire
GU32 2EW
GREAT BRITAIN
Tel: +44 (0)1730 233870

Email: enquiries@harriman-house.com
Website: www.harriman-house.com

First published in Great Britain in 2014.
Copyright © Harriman House Ltd.

The right of George Cooper to be identified as the Author has been asserted in accordance with the Copyright, Designs and Patents Act 1988.

ISBN: 9780857193827

British Library Cataloguing in Publication Data
A CIP catalogue record for this book can be obtained from the British Library.

Printed and bound in the United States of America by
Edwards Brothers Malloy

"And money is like muck, not good except it be spread."

Francis Bacon (1561–1626)

Thank you to Yasmeen and Nadia for provoking me into writing this book, to Ghadir for everything and to Vish for his invaluable help with the bloodwork.

CONTENTS

FREE EBOOK VERSION

As a buyer of the print book of *Money, Blood and Revolution* you can now download the eBook version free of charge to read on an eBook reader, your smartphone or your computer. Simply go to:

http://ebooks.harriman-house.com/moneybloodrevolution

or point your smartphone at the QRC below.

You can then register and download your free eBook.

FOLLOW US, LIKE US, EMAIL US

@HarrimanHouse
www.linkedin.com/company/harriman-house
www.facebook.com/harrimanhouse
contact@harriman-house.com

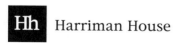 Harriman House

LIST OF FIGURES

ABOUT THE AUTHOR

Dr George Cooper has worked for Goldman Sachs, Deutsche Bank, J.P. Morgan and BlueCrest Capital Management in both fund management and investment strategy roles.

George's first book, *The Origin of Financial Crises*, received critical acclaim for its clear explanation of the monetary policy errors leading up to the global financial crisis.

Prior to joining the City, George worked as a research scientist at Durham University.

He lives in London with his wife and two children.

PREFACE

ABOUT 500 YEARS ago a middle ranking church official working in an obscure part of what is now northern Poland imagined a new way to think about the workings of the universe. Before Copernicus, mankind knew that the earth sat motionless at the very centre of the universe with the sun and the stars turning around it. After Copernicus, we knew the earth was just a minor planet orbiting an unremarkable star.

What Copernicus thought about the universe was important – it turned astrology into the science of astronomy – but *how* Copernicus thought about the universe was immeasurably more important. Copernicus taught us how to do science. He taught us to look for simple answers to complex problems and he showed us the importance of using our imagination.

Copernicus was the first of the scientific revolutionaries, but he was not the last. He has been followed by a long and glorious list of imitators. These copycat revolutionaries borrowed his scientific methods and to a surprising degree also used very similar imaginative tricks to turn their own fields into sciences.

William Harvey, the doctor of King Charles I, reimagined the flow of blood around the body. He made the human machine easier to understand, and in doing so turned medicine away from superstition and towards science.

Charles Darwin and Alfred Wallace imagined the evolution of species and modern scientific biology was born.

Alfred Wegener reimagined the workings of the earth. He imagined entire floating continents drifting around the world. In doing so, he fixed the confusion in geology – allowing this field also to graduate to the science faculty.

The first section of this book is about these four great scientific revolutions: why they became necessary and how they happened. It is about learning the tricks of Copernicus, Harvey, Darwin and Wegener. These great men all worked in very similar ways.

The second section of the book is about economics. First, about drawing parallels between the confused state of economics today and the state of astronomy, medicine, biology and geology prior to their revolutions. It is then about trying to fix the confusion in economics with the tricks of the great scientific revolutionaries. This section is about trying to find a new way to think about how economies work that could help turn economics into a true science.

The history of scientific revolutions shows that the leaders of a field almost always resist new ways of thinking, whereas younger students and interested laymen are often receptive to new ideas. This is especially true when the idea makes the field easier to understand. History also shows that it is the students and the laymen who then drive the new ideas forward in the face of resistance from the old order. For this reason I have written this book very much for the layman rather than for the professional economist.

I am told that chapter 7 contains the most difficult material. I would encourage readers not to be put off by this. Chapter 7 is a brief survey of just some of the numerous competing schools of economic thought. Today economics is a profoundly confused field, so any survey of it is inevitably going to be a little confusing. If chapter 7 leaves you scratching your head you have probably understood it quite well! If I have done my job properly much of this confusion should be lifted by the subsequent chapters.

The primary aim of this book is to find a better way to think about our economies. It is not about providing excuses to radically change our economic system. I hope to disappoint anyone looking for extreme ideas.

If there is a secondary aim to the book it is to help preserve our economic system and to protect it from some of the surprisingly extreme ideas buried within today's mainstream economic theories.

On a personal note, I must thank my daughters for prodding me into writing this book. The original idea came out of a discussion we had a few years ago over which subjects they should study at school. When they asked me about studying economics I rather too flippantly advised them against it. I think I said something like: economics is all confused, it will only teach you to think about the world in the wrong way. This led them to ask me a simple question: *What's wrong with economics?* This book is my attempt to answer their question and to discuss a few interesting bits of science along the way. It is written for them, but I hope it is of interest to others.

George Cooper
December 2013

1 INTRODUCTION:
THE BROKEN SCIENCE

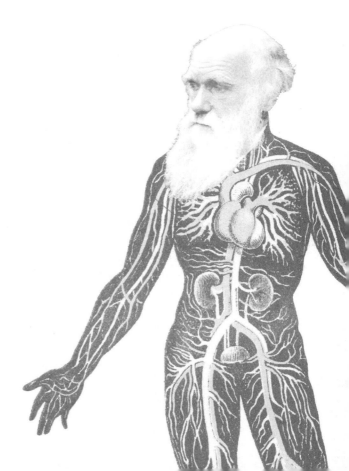

"The opposite of a correct statement is a false statement. The opposite of a profound truth may well be another profound truth."

Niels Bohr (1885–1962)

1.1 To Crash Now or Later?

CONSIDER THE FOLLOWING scenario. You are an airline pilot charged with flying a planeload of passengers across the Atlantic. You are offered the choice of two different aircraft. The first aircraft has been prepared by chief engineer Keynes and the second by chief engineer Hayek.

You have to choose which plane to use, so naturally you ask the advice of the two engineers. Keynes urges you to use his aircraft, offering a convincing explanation of why Hayek's plane will crash on take-off. Hayek urges you to use his aircraft, offering an equally convincing explanation of why Keynes's plane will crash upon landing.

At a loss as to which plane to choose, you seek the advice of two leading independent experts – Karl Marx and Adam Smith. Marx reassures you that it does not matter which aircraft you choose as both will inevitably suffer catastrophic failure. Similarly, Smith also reassures you that it does not matter which aircraft you choose, so long as you allow your chosen craft to fly itself.

This is a ridiculous scenario but it is not far from the choices and advice policymakers were faced with in the aftermath of the recent financial crisis.

As a result of the crisis, government spending surged, driven higher by rising unemployment benefits and the costs of bailing out the struggling financial system. At the same time, tax revenues plummeted as capital gains and corporate profits evaporated. With falling revenue and rising expenditure, governments around the world began running huge deficits, sending their already bloated borrowing levels ever higher.

One school of experts, the pro-stimulus camp, urged policymakers to increase their spending still further, thereby pushing debt levels ever higher. Their opponents, the pro-austerity camp, urged exactly the opposite policy of reducing government debt levels by cutting back on government spending. Meanwhile almost everyone in both camps agreed it was a good idea to pump trillions of dollars of freshly printed money into the financial markets.

The pro-stimulus camp explained that austerity would lead to an immediate economic crash as economies would enter a self-reinforcing economic contraction. This was the crash on take-off argument. The alternative pro-austerity camp explained that excess debt had caused the crisis in the first place and therefore adding even more debt would just make the inevitable next crash even more dangerous. This was the crash upon landing argument.

Our imaginary airline pilot at least had the option of refusing to fly either of the aircraft. Policymakers were not blessed with this opt-out. Some chose austerity – Greece, Spain, Portugal and Ireland, for example – though strictly speaking they had that option chosen for them. Others, most notably the United States and later Japan, chose stimulus. Britain, I would suggest, chose to preach austerity while practising stimulus.

Today the pro-stimulus camp is already claiming victory, supported by the evidence of the economic collapse that has occurred in the countries that chose austerity. In both Greece and Spain, the general unemployment level has come close to 30%, while youth unemployment is much higher again. It is reasonable to describe these unlucky economies as being already in a state of full-blown economic depression.

Meanwhile the economies that adopted stimulus policies are still barrelling down the runway hoping to reach take-off speed but struggling under the weight of an ever-growing debt load. As yet it is far from clear whether these economies will become airborne before reaching the end of the runway, so even these relative successes may yet end in tears.

1.2 Big Government, Small Government or Both?

Prior to the global financial crisis of 2008 there was near unanimity on how a modern economy worked and how it should be managed. The policy advice emanating from the economics profession was overwhelmingly in support of an efficient market laissez-faire model of economic management.

According to this school of thought, the nimble private sector was significantly more efficient than the lumbering government sector. Governments invariably destroyed value by spending money less effectively than their private-sector counterparts. Taxes acted to distort and discourage the productive entrepreneurial spirit of the private sector. And regulations could only impede the inherently efficient operation of a naturally stable free market system. According to this world view, the job of government was to step aside and let the private sector run the show. Small government, low taxes and deregulation was what the economics profession prescribed in order to optimally run our economies. Put differently, governments were told to adopt a policy of benign neglect.

By and large, in the three decades prior to the 2008 financial crisis, governments around the world – led by the example set in America and the UK – followed the advice of the academics. Taxes were cut, regulation was rolled back and the private sector was allowed to get on with its business largely free of government interference. Credit was allowed to grow unchecked.

But this small-government efficient-market philosophy is only one half of the story. At the same time the economics profession was pushing the small-government agenda they were also actively promoting the idea that monetary policy should be used to manage economic activity. Specifically, it was argued that monetary policy should be eased in order to stimulate more borrowing whenever economic growth was deemed to be inadequate. The central bankers, whose job it was to fix each and every economic problem with these monetary policies, became the rock stars of the financial world.

In effect academia was speaking out of two sides of its mouth at the same time. The laissez-faire efficient market philosophy was pushing governments to stay out of the process of economic management, while the philosophy of activist monetary policy was demanding ever more economic management. Of course, in practice, the policies of macroeconomic management through monetary policy were implemented via nominally independent central banks. The independence of the central banks provided a very small, unconvincing fig leaf to save the embarrassment of those who managed to advocate both activist monetary policy and minimalist government interference at the same time. Nevertheless, this inconsistency was obvious to many.

This unfortunate state of affairs meant that governments administered monetary policy so as to encourage the private sector to borrow without limit while at the same time rolling back any regulatory constraints on borrowing levels. The result of this strange combination of big-government monetary policy married to small-government regulatory policy was the biggest credit bubble in history. This credit bubble burst in spectacular fashion in 2008, causing the global financial crisis.

1.3 From Malign Neglect to Policy Paralysis

It would have been reasonable to expect the global financial crisis to trigger a wholesale reappraisal of both the economic theories and economic policies that led up to the crisis. In practice this has not happened. It is now more than five years since the crisis rocked the global economy and what can we say has changed?

There has been some minor tinkering with the regulation of the banking system and financial markets but, at least to this observer, these are no more than cosmetic adjustments and will make little difference to the system overall. More importantly, there has been no effort at all to seriously reconsider how monetary policy was used in the run-up to the crisis. Instead, our central bankers have redoubled their efforts to encourage ever greater leverage within asset markets by deploying multi-trillion-dollar quantitative easing programs. No doctor would expect to cure an alcoholic by advising he drink even more whisky, but our monetary policies appear to be attempting to cure one debt bubble with an even greater debt bubble.

It is reasonable to ask ourselves how this strange state of affairs has come about. After the biggest financial crisis in history, why have we continued to deploy the same policies that originally caused the crisis?

It is tempting to look for individuals or groups of individuals to blame for both the original financial crisis and for the failure to reform policy subsequent to the crisis. While superficially satisfying, this may be a fool's errand. The real culprit may be within the 'science' of economics itself.

Prior to the global financial crisis there was a broad, if misguided, consensus within the economics profession describing how to manage the economy. After the crisis this comfortable consensus was ruptured as various leading economists began openly disagreeing with one another and advising very different sets of policies. Nowhere is this better demonstrated than by the long-running argument between the pro-stimulus and pro-austerity schools. And this debate is itself best exemplified by the long-running spat between the two intellectual heavyweights of Paul Krugman and Niall Ferguson.

For years now the Nobel Prize-winning economist Paul Krugman and the Harvard historian Niall Ferguson have been slugging it out in a running public battle over how best to deal with the financial crisis. The academic credentials of both of these two gentlemen are impeccable. They are both clearly intelligent, articulate and persuasive; both have well-thought-out reasons for their positions. Nevertheless both advocate diametrically opposite policies – Krugman argues for more government spending, while Ferguson argues for less.

It would be a mistake to dismiss the Krugman-Ferguson row as just a clash of egos between two academics. Firstly, it is not just an argument between two individuals: it is the public manifestation of a fissure running right through the field of economics. Secondly, the argument is not confined to academia. Recently the American federal government was forced into partial closure due to an argument between the Republicans and Democrats over raising the ceiling on the amount of money that the American government was permitted to borrow. At its heart, the cause of the federal shutdown was the same as the argument over austerity vs stimulus that is playing out between Krugman and Ferguson. An analogous situation is occurring in Europe with a deep policy divide between the German-led pro-austerity camp pitted against the southern countries suffering the consequences of the austerity policies.

In the five years since the global financial crisis occurred and the austerity vs stimulus debate began, Krugman and Ferguson have landed minor blows on one another but neither has delivered the knock-out punch necessary to win the argument. If anything, their respective positions appear to be more entrenched than ever. The same can be said of the rift between the Republicans and Democrats.

The impasse within academia seems to be resulting in a similar impasse between policymakers, the result of which is, by default, a continuation of previous economic and monetary policies. As a result, the policy environment today is largely indistinguishable from that which was in place prior to the financial crisis. Put differently, the global financial crisis has seen the economics profession transit from a state of pre-crisis complacency to post-crisis confusion, and the economic and monetary policies of our governments transit from pre-crisis negligence to post-crisis paralysis.

1.4 Self-contradictory Truths

Looked at objectively, the arguments of the pro-austerity and pro-stimulus camps are both persuasive. Paul Krugman was right in warning of the devastating consequences of austerity. Right now there are millions of unemployed young people in southern Europe whose lives are being blighted by the sudden shift of their government's fiscal policies. Equally, Niall Ferguson was also right in insisting that we could not expect the policies that caused the crisis to cure it. At the moment the countries pursuing fiscal stimulus are still accumulating debt at a faster rate than their economies are growing. Unless the growth rates of these countries suddenly improves relative to the growth rate of their debts, the laws of arithmetic will inevitably triumph over the hopes of policymakers – making default or monetisation inevitable.

The uncomfortable truth is that while stimulus policies have certainly eased the pain in the near term, they have not produced the economic growth expected of them – and have therefore not become self-funding and sustainable.

It is easy to become exasperated with the inability of our elected policymakers to work together to determine a path out of the crisis. But we should also have some sympathy with their predicament. In large part our policymakers are taking their cue from the advice being offered by academic economists. Currently they are being fed a lot of very inconsistent messages. It appears that the 'science' of economics is unable to resolve the Krugman-Ferguson debate and is unable to provide coherent guidance for policymakers.

Indeed I would go further than this and argue that the science of economics first failed policymakers in providing the wrong advice prior to the financial crisis and is now failing policymakers in providing, in aggregate, no advice after the crisis. We may have a crisis within our economies, but the source of this crisis lies within the 'science' of economics.

1.5 We Have an Interesting Problem

Prior to the financial crisis, mainstream economic thinking argued simultaneously for small government – on taxation, regulation and spending – but big government on monetary policy. After the financial crisis, economics is now also arguing simultaneously for more government spending and for less government spending. Just look at the latest Nobel

Prize in economics, which was shared between three economists: Eugene Fama, Lars Hansen and Robert Shiller. It is not too much of an oversimplification to say that Fama was awarded his prize for explaining that markets are efficient and Shiller was awarded his for explaining that they are not efficient. Economics currently exists in a kind of Alice in Wonderland state, able to believe multiple, seemingly inconsistent, things at the same time.

The recent award of the Nobel Prize to both Shiller and Fama triggered a mini debate in the press over whether this meant that economics was qualified to be called a real science or not. I confess to having been rather happy to see this question being aired as it is an issue that is central to many of the following chapters. The starting premise of this book is that the internal inconsistencies between economic theories, the apparently unresolvable debates between economists and the incoherent economic policies of our governments, are not reasons to classify economics as being unscientific. Rather, these are reasons to believe that economics is a science that has entered a state of crisis.

This crisis is, I believe, not a chaotic, incomprehensible crisis; rather it is a well-understood scientific crisis of the type that has bedevilled every other science at one time or another throughout history. The good news is that, thanks to the work of scientist and philosopher Thomas Kuhn, scientific crises are well-researched and well-understood.

The purpose of the rest of this book is to explore the idea that economics is in a state of scientific crisis and to look at both the work of Thomas Kuhn and the lessons of other scientific crises to provide hints as to how it may be possible for economics to find a way out of its crisis.

The first section of this book, chapters 2 through 6, is concerned with explaining what a scientific crisis is and what is necessary to get out of a state of scientific crisis. Chapter 2 discusses the nature and structure of scientific revolutions as described by Thomas Kuhn. Chapters 3 to 6 discuss four examples of famous scientific revolutions from history. These are, respectively, the Copernican revolution in astronomy, William Harvey's discovery of the circulatory motion of blood in the body, Charles

Darwin's theory of evolution, and finally Alfred Wegener's theory of continental drift.

At first sight readers may be forgiven for wondering what these chapters are doing in a book on economics. Hopefully by the end of the book their purpose will have been made clear. In the meantime, however, I would note that the history of science shows that, to a surprising degree, ideas from one science frequently help resolve problems in another. I have included all of these stories because I believe they help shed light on the crisis within the science of economics.

Chapter 7 contains a review of some of the various competing schools of economic thought. The purpose of this chapter is to make the case that the field of economics today bears a striking similarity to the state of astronomy prior to the Copernican revolution, medicine prior to Harvey's discovery of circulatory blood flow, biology prior to Darwin's theory of evolution and even to geology before Wegener's idea of continental drift. Chapter 7 is therefore an attempt to persuade readers that economics is in a state of scientific crisis and is thus ripe for one of Thomas Kuhn's scientific revolutions as described in Chapter 2.

Chapters 8 and 9 are both concerned with finding the resolution to the crisis of economics – that is to say, with identifying the paradigm shift in the way we think about our economic system that will help resolve many of the internal inconsistencies between the various schools of economic thought. The purpose of chapters 8 and 9 is therefore to help us start looking at the economic system in a way that lets us move beyond the austerity vs stimulus clash. These chapters will, I hope, help readers see more clearly the conditions necessary to achieve robust economic growth and also to understand how some of the policies of the last few decades have inadvertently undermined economic growth.

Chapter 10 then looks at the policy implications of the model presented in chapter 9. In this chapter I discuss specific areas of fiscal and monetary policy that, I believe, must be reformed in order to progressively return our economic system to a balanced condition, where it is able to generate growth without relying on the artificial support of government stimulus.

Doubtless the implications of the model presented in chapter 9 and the consequent policy reforms that flow from it in chapter 10 will cause unease in some quarters – whenever monetary and fiscal policies are adjusted there are winners and losers. That said, economic policy is not a zero-sum game. If we get it right, in the long run everyone can win; if we get it wrong, everyone can lose. It is my hope that by finding a new way to look at the origins of economic growth we can get closer to a consensus on the policies necessary for everyone to win.

PART **SCIENCE**

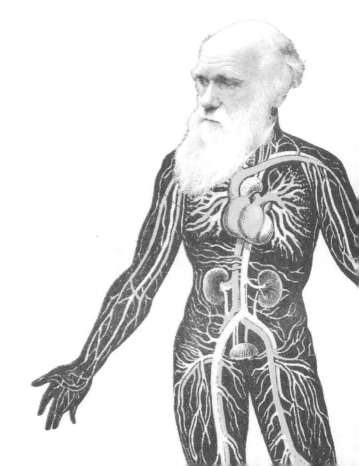

2 SCIENTIFIC REVOLUTIONS

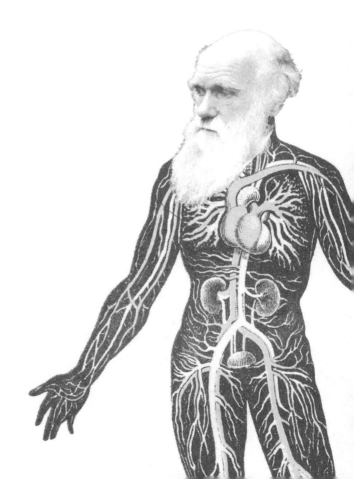

"It doesn't matter how beautiful your theory is, it doesn't matter how smart you are. If it doesn't agree with experiment, it's wrong."

Richard Feynman (1918–1988)

2.1 Thomas S. Kuhn

THIS BOOK HAS been inspired by the work of Thomas Kuhn, and you will be hearing a lot about his ideas in its pages. Kuhn lived from 1922 to 1996. He worked at a number of top US universities, including Harvard, Berkeley, Princeton and MIT. Kuhn is a difficult man to pigeonhole. He started out as a physicist, became a student of the history of science and then arguably morphed into a philosopher. I prefer to think of him as a scientist of science. By this I mean, he tried to understand how the process of science works in practice. His work is especially valuable in explaining how a science can get stuck, becoming unable to move forward, and then how it can get unstuck, allowing sudden dramatic progress.

Kuhn studied and wrote about scientific discovery across a whole range of fields and published his findings in a famous book, *The Structure of Scientific Revolutions* (Kuhn, 1962). Kuhn's book has been rated as one of the top 100 most influential books of the 20th century. And rather upsettingly for scientists, Kuhn found that science is often not very scientific at all.

2.1.1 The problem of incommensurability

Kuhn identified a key problem in the way science works and promptly gave it the horrible name of *incommensurability*.[1] The problem he found was that the way we analyse and interpret the world and look at

---

[1] The dictionary definitions of incommensurability talk of it being a condition in which things are impossible to compare or measure in a common way.

experimental data is intimately entwined with our existing, pre-conceived understanding of how the world works.

As a result, one group of observers will look at a given set of data and interpret that data to mean one thing, while another group looking at the same data may see it as meaning something quite different. Often the different groups are working to sets of assumptions – Kuhn used the term paradigms – that are so different that they are simply unable to understand how the other groups have reached their differing conclusions. When this happens, Kuhn said, the different perceptions of each group are *incommensurable*, making it impossible for the groups to communicate effectively. One way to illustrate Kuhn's problem is to consider the following famous picture.

Figure 1: One picture with two possible interpretations

If you are told, before you look at this picture, that it shows an old woman staring into the bottom left of the frame, then in all likelihood you will see the old woman. On the other hand, if you are told it is a picture of a young lady looking away from you, staring into the distance, then you will likely see the young lady. Both are quite reasonable interpretations of the picture, but both are quite inconsistent with each other.

Now imagine two art critics were given the job of reviewing this picture. One happened to see the old lady, while the other saw the younger lady. The two reviews would be quite different. Neither critic would be able to understand why the other's review was so different. As the two critics had, in effect, seen two different pictures, they simply would not be able to reconcile their positions and establish a working dialogue. Quite likely they would both end up concluding the other was an idiot.

In Kuhn's language, the two reviews would be incommensurable with one another. That is to say, incompatible and – importantly – incomparable. Despite their obvious inconsistency, it would be impossible to define either as objectively more or less correct than the other. The only way to reconcile the two is to move away from either the old lady paradigm or the young lady paradigm and to shift to a new perspective recognising the validity of both views. In this case the new paradigm is to accept that the picture is an optical illusion.[2]

You can see another real example of this problem every time you are lucky enough to see a clear, starry sky at night. Prior to the Copernican revolution, the topic of the next chapter, people believed that the stars were something akin to bright jewels embedded on the inside surface of a giant black sphere. This sphere was believed to encircle and spin around the earth. When looking at the stars with this paradigm in mind, the ancients saw the night sky as a giant, beautifully decorated dome above

---

[2] For those interested in the philosophy of science, Kuhn's analysis of the process of developing understanding has parallels with the ancient idea of the dialectic as practised by Plato – the idea being to improve understanding by finding a way to reconcile views that appear to be both individually valid and also inconsistent. The German philosopher Hegel expressed a similar idea, arguing that understanding progresses by finding the synthesis of a thesis and its antithesis.

their heads. Today, of course, we 'know' that the stars are bright suns, scattered at great distances from us throughout space. But the next time you are outside on a clear night, try looking at the sky as a giant black dome decorated with glowing jewels; the picture is surprisingly convincing. You can see the stars as jewels on a dome or as balls of gas scattered through space but, like the picture of the two women, it's very difficult to hold both images in your mind at the same time.

This is a good way to understand Kuhn's problem of incommensurability. All too often what we see in the data is what we expect to see – what our paradigm or prior assumptions condition us to see – and we cannot understand why those working to different paradigms see different things.

Kuhn explained that when a science becomes a battlefield between different and incommensurable world views, it moves into a state of crisis. Neither school of thought can triumph as neither can convince the other of the validity of its position. As a result, progress stalls and confusion sets in.

In economics, where the interpretation of data is subjective and we are never quite sure of how to disentangle cause from effect, the problem of incommensurability is rife. For example, consider the following quote from the political scientist Charles Murray:

> "You can easily find evidence on behalf of social democracy (given that pair of priorities) that you think is dispositive. I look at the same evidence and judge it to be peripheral, irrelevant, or wrong-headed – not because the numbers are wrong, but because of differences on first principles...so our positions largely pass in the night, neither directly in conflict with the other."

In other words, in economics it is quite common for people to agree about the data but disagree entirely about what the data means.

In chapter 7 it will be argued that economics has fractured into so many competing, incommensurable, schools of thought that it should now be considered to be in a state of scientific crisis.

2.2 Two Flavours of Science: Mr Spock vs Captain Kirk

Kuhn argued that science progresses in two distinct ways. As with so many things in life, these are best explained with reference to *Star Trek*. Trekkies will be aware that the storylines of the classic *Star Trek* episodes often revolved around the dynamic between Captain James T. Kirk and Mr Spock as they confronted some seemingly insoluble problem. On one side there was the emotionless, relentlessly rational Mr Spock. For Spock, every answer to a problem must be arrived at through cold, hard, deductive logic. On the other side there was Captain Kirk, the imaginative, instinctive, and frequently illogical genius. For Kirk, problems were solved by intuition, and the details worked out later. Invariably, when the problem arose, Kirk would make the intuitive leap toward the solution, with Spock protesting: "But that is illogical, Captain."[3]

Traditionally we think scientists work like Mr Spock. Observations are made, experiments are performed, data is collected and analysed. Theories are developed to explain the data and new experiments are made to test these theories. If the data agrees with the theory, the theory is thought to be supported; if it does not, then the theory is corrected until it fits the data. New theories evolve as refinements of old theories in a steady progression, always being made to accord with the experimental, empirical evidence. If the theories cannot be made to fit the evidence, they are discarded and new ones sought.

---

[3] Note I am referring here to the vintage 1960s television series. To get an appreciation of the subtlety of the Spock vs Kirk dynamic, only the original William Shatner and Leonard Nimoy material will do. The modern frat-boy reinterpretation of the franchise is quite unsuitable for advanced philosophical musings.

This view of the scientific process is known as the 'empirical method' or the 'Baconian method', after the 16th-century philosopher Francis Bacon, who was an early proponent of experimentation.[4] The Baconian method is responsible for what is known as the 'empirical test'. This is science's most fundamental rule, which states that above all else theories must fit the facts. Science's second most fundamental rule is the principle of parsimony, which states that theories should be as simple as possible.

Kuhn did not dispute the central role of the empirical test in science. He just issued an important warning – make sure you're aware that the theory you're using is dictating what you are choosing to look at and how you interpret what you see. If your theory tells you the lights in the night sky are jewels on a dome, you will see jewels on a dome, and you may measure their different luminosities and from this deduce their relative sizes. If your theory tells you the lights are suns scattered through space, you will see suns and may measure their different luminosities and from this deduce their relative distances from earth.

This is where Kuhn made one of his most insightful observations. By recognising that our theories define our observations, he explained that the story we tell ourselves about the way the world works can dominate and define our observations of the world. This realisation of the importance of the story, or theory, then allowed Kuhn to explain how a science that is stuck in a crisis can get out of the crisis.

According to Kuhn, the way out of a scientific crisis almost always requires the Captain Kirk approach. What is needed is an intuitive leap, a paradigm shift, toward a new model that leads to interpreting our

---

[4] Francis Bacon is widely credited with being one of the first philosophers to articulate and publicise the modern empirical scientific method. Bacon emphasised the importance of checking theories against experimental evidence and the importance of publishing results so that they could benefit society as a whole and be confirmed by others. Bacon was also one of the first scientists to lay down his life for his beliefs. He died shortly after catching a cold, while stuffing a dead chicken with snow, on Hampstead Heath. He was testing his theory that ice could be used to preserve dead flesh. Interestingly, there is a long running conspiracy theory suggesting that Francis Bacon was the true author of the plays of William Shakespeare. Part of the evidence for this conspiracy relates to William Harvey, who we shall meet in chapter 4. We'll also return to the Shakespeare conspiracy theory in chapter 4.

observations in a different way. According to Kuhn, you just don't get to the breakthrough through ever-closer inspection of the data using the old paradigms. In at least three of the four scientific revolutions discussed in the next chapters, the breakthroughs did not involve any new observations – rather, they involved reinterpretations. As a result of Kuhn's work, we now call these shifts in perspective 'paradigm shifts'.

Rather depressingly, Kuhn also showed that through the process of a scientific revolution scientists don't behave very much like scientists at all. Before the paradigm shift they cling doggedly to obviously false theories regardless of the experimental evidence. After the paradigm shift they often try to defend their discredited ideas in a most ungentlemanly fashion.

At the risk of oversimplifying Kuhn's work, I have recast his description of a scientific revolution as a play in five acts. Though in practice it's not quite a play, as the acts often run in part concurrently.

Act I – The Discrepancies Show

The first stage of the scientific revolution is when the prevailing paradigm begins to fail the empirical test. That is to say the experimental evidence and the predictions of the scientific models part company. Over time the discrepancies accumulate until it becomes apparent that the models need fixing in some way.

Act II – The Disagreements Start

Once the disagreements with reality become apparent, the experts begin to cast around for ways to fix their theories. Naturally, they resist discarding their old models entirely and instead look for small ad-hoc fixes. This is where the trouble starts.

Different groups try to solve different discrepancies with different ad-hoc fixes. Each group has its own pet ideas and follows its own independent research agenda. Over time the field splinters into many competing schools of thought. Each school tends to focus on different problems, develop different models and interpret data in different ways.

The schools seek to redefine the scope of the field around their own paradigms, in effect trying to delegitimise competing schools. The longer the state of confusion persists, the more complex and fragmented the field becomes. Finally the paradigms of the competing schools become irreconcilable; the problem of incommensurability sets in as progress in the whole field grinds to a halt.

Kuhn observed that in this phase the leaders of the different competing schools of thought almost never reject their paradigms based on observation. No matter how obviously wrong their models become, they retain their faith and continue trying to tweak their ideas. In short, scientists behave in a very human way – they sacrifice scientific integrity in order to preserve personal fiefdoms.

As we shall see in the next chapter, this phase can be very drawn out: even judged conservatively, astronomy spent 2,000 years in a state of internal disagreement. Within economics the internal conflicts have been raging for well over a century.

Act III – The Revolution

Eventually a new paradigm emerges that resolves many of the problems of the field. This new paradigm involves a shift in perspective, which allows a reinterpretation of existing knowledge. It manages to retain the best of the old thinking and integrates apparently conflicting views into a new coherent model. This is the stage known as the paradigm shift.

Act IV – The Rejection

Now comes the backlash stage. The paradigm shift is rejected and ridiculed by the incumbent leaders of the field. This is one of the most reliably repeatable stages of a scientific revolution. Often the old guard becomes frustrated that the new idea cannot be derived logically from their own theories and did not arise as the result of new observations. Because the old leaders of the field never change their minds, this phase lasts for at least a period of several decades until the old guard retires, dies out, or fades away.

Act V – The Acceptance

The new theory is adopted gradually as younger, more open-minded scientists, who study the new paradigm early in their careers, become leaders of the field. Kuhn's final blow to the ego of scientists was his observation that the vanguard of the new paradigm is usually led by non-expert outsiders. These outsiders are often thoroughly frustrated with the confusion of the old order and eager to accept the clarity of a new idea.

2.3 Kuhn's Analysis and Economics

Kuhn's analysis of scientific revolutions is relevant to economics in a number of ways. His observation that we do not discard theories based on their failure to describe reality is especially pertinent. Many people, myself included, have long wondered at the ability of the neoclassical economic orthodoxy – which describes our economies as docile self-stabilising systems free of boom-bust cycles or asset-price bubbles – to survive in the face of endless experimental refutations. Kuhn's analysis suggests an answer to this conundrum: no matter how discredited a theory becomes, it will never be rejected until a better theory comes along. In short, it's not enough to point out that economics is failing or even *how* it is failing. If things are to improve, we must first find a better model to replace the old paradigm.

For those of us who think economic theory has gone awry, the message from Kuhn's analysis is blunt: don't waste your time criticising the old ideas; go out and find some better ones. Then wait at least 30 years for the new ideas to take hold!

3 A CRISIS IN THE HEAVENS

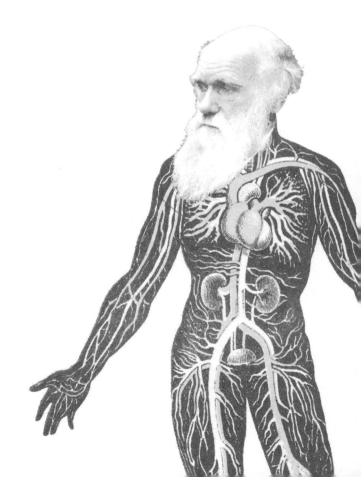

"If the Lord Almighty had consulted me before embarking on creation, I should have recommended something simpler."

King Alfonso X, commenting on the Ptolemaic model of the universe

3.1 Copernicus – The First and Most Important Revolutionary

THE COPERNICAN REVOLUTION has the distinction of being the first, by far the most protracted, and irrefutably the most important of all scientific revolutions. By demonstrating that it was possible to improve on the knowledge of the ancient scholars, Copernicus reawakened the spirit of scientific inquiry and kick-started the entire scientific age.

Copernicus lived between 1473–1543. Aside from his years of study in Italy, he spent his entire life in northern Poland. He was lucky enough to be born into a well-connected family of wealthy merchants and senior officials in the Catholic Church. He studied mathematics, astronomy, medicine and especially canon law, first in Poland and later in what were Europe's, and therefore the world's, top universities, at Padua and Bologna.

Copernicus was no child prodigy: he was already 30 years old by the time he returned from his studies to become secretary and doctor to his uncle, the Bishop of Warmia. Despite his extensive education and good connections, Copernicus never achieved high office in the church and lived out his life as a middle-ranking church official. Most likely, he was too distracted by heavenly bodies to crawl up the career ladder.[5]

---

[5] There is some evidence that Copernicus suffered a protracted losing battle with his vow of chastity which may have held back his Church career. Jack Repcheck's *Copernicus' Secret* gives an entertaining non-technical account of the human side of the Copernican revolution (Repcheck, 2009).

3.2 Early Astronomical Models

To understand the importance of the Copernican revolution, it is necessary to go back to some of the earliest models of the universe. The first recognisably scientific theory of the universe was the two-sphere model, which dates back at least a few thousand years BC. As the name suggests, this simple model involved just two spheres. The earth was the inner sphere and it was believed to be surrounded by an outer celestial sphere or shell. As mentioned previously, stars were believed to be shining jewels or flames fixed to the inside surface of the outer sphere. The outer sphere was believed to rotate around the earth, carrying the stars with it while the earth remained motionless.

This simple model had a number of attractive scientific properties. It involved just one moving part, making it pleasingly simple. Had the principle of parsimony been thought of then, it would have fitted nicely. It explained why all of the stars appeared to move together. It also explained why the image of the night sky varied according to the latitude of the observer – observers at different latitudes would see different portions of the celestial sphere.

The two most glaring, or rather glowing, problems with the two-sphere model were of course the sun and the moon. These did not move with the stars on the celestial sphere. Rather annoyingly, the sun took 24 hours to move around the earth, while the celestial sphere and its stars revolved just slightly faster, in 23 hours and 56 minutes to be precise. The near coincidence of these two rotation speeds was known, but it was not thought terribly significant in ancient times.

Naturally the ancient astronomers could not just ignore the sun and the moon, so they enhanced their model by placing each of these bodies on their own individual spheres. This enhancement to the two-sphere model was the start of a long slippery slope that was to send astronomy and science generally down a very dark alley for several thousand years.

This new model – we'll call it the four-sphere model – added a lot of extra complexity to explain the motions of just two, admittedly important, objects. The complexity did not stop there. Being a four-sphere model, with the stars on the outer shell, it was necessary to explain how we could see through the inner spheres to the stars on the outer sphere. This was fixed with another assumption – the spheres carrying the heavenly bodies were made of perfectly transparent crystal.

Figure 2: A simple four-sphere model of the universe

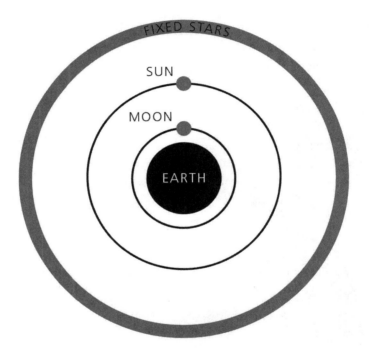

3.2.1 The problem of the wandering stars

With evening entertainment being somewhat limited in ancient times, there was little to do at night other than watch these celestial spheres turning slowly overhead. As a result it was noticed that five of the stars did not behave as they should. These five stars moved at a different speed to all of the others and at different speeds to each other. Reflecting their special nature they were given individual names – Mercury, Venus, Mars, Jupiter and Saturn – and collectively called the planets, a term derived from the Greek for wandering star.

Obviously this was a problem for the four-sphere model of the universe as the wandering stars did not fit on any of the spheres. Aristotle (384–322 BC) stepped in and fixed the problem of the planets with a further enhancement. His solution was, naturally enough, to add another five rotating spheres, each one carrying its own wandering star. This took the total number of spheres to nine. Just for good measure he then added another sphere on the outside of the star-encrusted celestial sphere. This outer sphere was supposed to act as a sort of drive-wheel for the whole system and was known as the prime-mover. With this final enhancement the model had ten heavenly spheres.

Figure 3: Aristotle's geocentric model of the universe

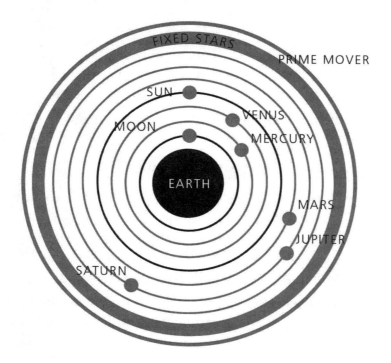

Aristotle's model was a clumsy affair requiring extravagant assumptions to explain small observations – whole spheres were used to carry mere pinpricks of light. In the language of Thomas Kuhn, Aristotle's model lacked conceptual efficiency. Nevertheless Aristotle's model carried the day. It was adopted by the mainstream and dominated astronomy up until the first century AD.

Aristotle's model may have dominated but it was by no means the only school of thought. Even before Aristotle, Leucippus (5th century BC) argued that the whole rotating-sphere paradigm was nonsense and described the universe as an infinite space, speckled with an infinite number of stars. Unfortunately this story did not win out. A little later Heraclides of Pontus (4th century BC) suggested the stars did not move at all and explained that their apparent motion was actually due to the rotation of the earth. This idea also fell by the wayside – another tragically missed opportunity. Finally, shortly after the time of Aristotle, Aristarchus of Samos (310–230 BC) proposed that the sun was at the centre of the solar system, with the earth and the planets revolving around it. Aristarchus had essentially achieved the Copernican breakthrough nearly two millennia before Copernicus. Had the Aristotelian nonsense not triumphed over the ideas of Aristarchus we might already have been well on the way to colonising the stars!

3.2.2 The problem of retrograde motion

The rejection of Aristarchus's superior model would have been forgivable were it not for the fact that even in Aristotle's time it was known that his inferior model was wrong. The problem was, again, the troublesome motion of the wandering stars, which were known to occasionally turn around and move in the opposite direction to the other stars. This odd behaviour was known as 'retrograde motion'. To further complicate the picture, the luminosity of the wandering stars was also known to change over time.

Eudoxus (408–355 BC) tried to explain the problem of retrograde motion with a model of extraordinary complexity. The sun and moon were placed on three interlinked moving spheres while the five planets each required four moving spheres. Even then Eudoxus's model could not explain the variable brightness of the planets. Mercifully this extravagant model did not gain support.

Given the prior knowledge of retrograde motion, Aristotle's model should never have made it off the drawing board. But it gained acceptance nevertheless and in doing so provided a fine example of how we are able to suppress experimental evidence in favour of a good story. The idea of the model, or the story, dominating the data is central to Kuhn's thesis.

3.2.3 Ptolemy's tragic triumph

If Aristotle's ten-sphere model of the universe was an unfortunate mistake then the subsequent triumph of the Ptolemaic model was nothing short of a scientific calamity. By the first century AD astronomers thought they had found a way to explain the retrograde motion and the variable brightness of the wandering stars. The answer, they thought, came with the invention of the idea of epicycles. This model is generally referred to as the Ptolemaic model, though it is unfair to assign Ptolemy (c.90–168 AD) all of the blame as the idea had been around for some time before he arrived on the scene.

The Ptolemaic model explained both the retrograde motion and the variable brightness of the planets with epicycles. The idea was that each of the planets described a compound motion made up of not one but two circular motions. The planet was placed on a smaller rotating sphere, the epicycle. The centre of this epicycle, the equant, was then placed on a larger rotating sphere, the deferent.

Figure 4: Ptolemy's explanation of retrograde motion with epicycles

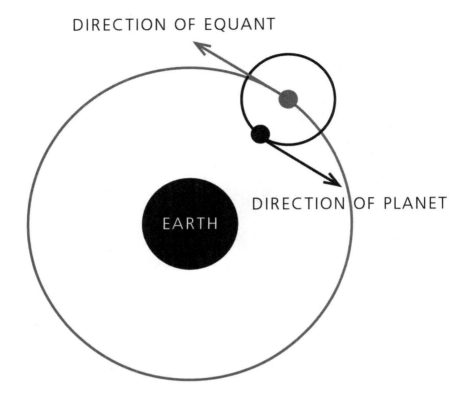

The deferent turned about the earth and the epicycle turned about the equant. The equant being somehow fixed to the deferent – little details like how the whole thing held together were glossed over. This model allowed the planets to change direction as they orbited the earth and to move toward and away from the earth. The former explained retrograde motion while the latter took care of variable brightness.

Ptolemy appeared to have fixed the problem of the wandering planets once and for all. But this fix came at a high price. As a result of Ptolemy's model the planets had acquired a highly complex motion. Ptolemy had twisted and folded Aristotle's elegant circular orbits into a bizarre, never-ending pretzel shape.

Figure 5: Ptolemy's complex pretzel-shaped planetary orbits

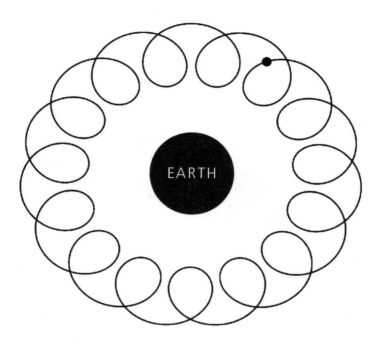

To make matters worse, even with these new complications Ptolemy's model still could not quite explain the real observed motions of the planets. Nevertheless, Ptolemy's epicycles offered the best story available at the time and displaced Aristotle's model as the new consensus.

The partial success of the Ptolemaic model was to have disastrous implications for astronomy and for science more broadly. In the first instance it sent astronomers on a path of building models of ever increasing complexity. Astronomers attempted to improve on the basic Ptolemaic model with additional compound epicycles and the axes of rotations of the spheres were offset allowing the creation of complex eccentric motions. The complexity of the models grew and the number of the models proliferated, but the explanatory power of these models failed to improve. Fortunately all of this was going on before computers had been invented. Heaven knows what mathematical monstrosities would have been conjured up had computers been around then.

Worse even than the complexity and inconsistency of the astronomical models was the fact that Ptolemy's twisted and folded pretzel orbits had no counterpart on earth. Ptolemy's model made it clear that there were different laws for the motions of the planets to those that described the behaviour of things on earth. There was no reason to imagine that universal physical laws might exist and therefore absolutely no reason to look for them. (Kuhn explained that the model we use defines the measurements we make and the questions we ask – once again the story dominates.)

After Ptolemy, astronomy became progressively more complex, less elegant and more fragmented. In the end astronomy degenerated into little more than a tool of astrology, rather than the engine of scientific advancement that it should have been.

To quote Kuhn:

> "During the 17 centuries that separate Hipparchus from Copernicus all the most creative practitioners of technical astronomy endeavoured to invent some new set of minor geometric modifications that would make the basic one-epicycle one-deferent technique precisely fit the observed motion of the planets."
>
> Kuhn, 1957

By this stage the field of astronomy was in full crisis. There was no single astronomical theory at all, just a collection of disparate models, each of which failed in its own particular way. Again from Kuhn:

> "No version of the [Ptolemaic] system ever quite withstood the test of additional refined observations, and this failure, combined with the total disappearance of the conceptual economy that had made cruder versions of the two-sphere universe so convincing, ultimately lead to the Copernican revolution."

After Ptolemy we would have to wait nearly one and a half millennia before Copernicus began unravelling Ptolemy's mess.

3.3 The Copernican Revolution

We now know that all of the early astronomical models derived from the foundations of the Aristotelian/Ptolemaic paradigm were doomed to fail. This is because they were all built upon a set of invalid axioms. Axioms are dangerous things in science. They are the very core ideas of a field upon which all other ideas are built, the foundations if you like, of a body of knowledge that is considered so self-evident it does not need to be checked or worried about.

Often the axioms of a field are implicitly assumed in the very earliest stages of a science's development. After a period of time they become buried so deep beneath the body of subsequent theory that later scientists are not even conscious that they are using the axioms at all. Usually axioms are correct, but when they are not the whole superstructure of a field can come crashing down. When Einstein developed his general theory of relativity he had to reject the axioms of Euclidian geometry. This meant rejecting the really basic self-evident truths that we all learn in school like the fact that there are 180 degrees in a triangle. After Einstein we now know that there are not 180 degrees in a triangle, at least not if there is mass around, which there always is.

For the astronomers working before Copernicus, the first flawed axiom they were working to was the idea that the earth was stationary, at the centre of the universe. The second flawed axiom was that all celestial motion was perfectly circular. The planets, it was assumed, could only move in a way described by combinations of perfect circles. Despite the rising complexity of their models and the failure of their field to progress for thousands of years, almost no astronomers questioned the assumptions of a geocentric universe with perfect circular motion. Even Copernicus himself only questioned one of these axioms.

By medieval standards, Copernicus lived a long life: he was 70 years old by the year of his death, 1543. This was also the year of the first publication of his great work on astronomy – *On the Revolutions of Heavenly Spheres*. It is said that he was handed a copy of the first edition as he lay on his deathbed and died that same day.

By 1543 Copernicus had spent nearly four decades performing astronomical observations and collecting data on the motions of the planets. Despite this there are compelling reasons to believe that none of his meticulous observations contributed to his revolutionary new theory of the solar system. We know this because Copernicus had actually published his theory in a short pamphlet, 'Commentariolus', at least three decades before the publication of his more famous work, and shortly after he had returned from university in Italy. Copernicus had done what Kuhn described – he had guessed at the new model, quite possibly while a student in Italy, and then spent a lifetime checking the data to see if he was right.[6]

All of the vital innovative elements of Copernicus's theory were clearly enunciated in the postulates of his earlier work, namely:

1. The moon orbits around the earth.

2. The planets orbit around the sun.

3. The distance between the earth and the sun is much smaller than between the earth and the stars.

4. The apparent motion of the stars is caused by the rotation of the earth.

5. The retrograde motion of the planets is caused by the earth's rotation about the sun.

The Copernican model was really nothing more than a shift of perspective. In his mind's eye Copernicus had placed himself on the sun and then reimagined the motion of the heavenly bodies from that new vantage point. Once he did this, suddenly the whole universe became much simpler.

---

[6] This is no accident as Kuhn's analysis of scientific revolutions was itself the result of his extensive research on the Copernican revolution. This chapter draws heavily upon Kuhn's *The Copernican Revolution* (Kuhn T. S., 1957).

It is worth noting that Copernicus had retained the incorrect assumption that the planets moved in perfectly circular orbits, which meant that his model was just as inaccurate as Ptolemy's. Indeed, for the purpose of predicting the motions of the planets they were mathematically equivalent. Copernicus's model did not lead to empirical precision. All it achieved was improved conceptual efficiency.

Copernicus's model was elegant; he had unfolded Ptolemy's pretzel-shaped orbits, shown that it was possible to improve on ideas handed down from Greek scholars, and exposed the bedrock for future scientific progress. Copernicus had worked intuitively, more like Captain Kirk than Mr Spock. The key was a little imagination, a small change in perspective and the confidence to question one of the cherished axioms of his field.

Figure 6: Copernicus's heliocentric model of the solar system with circular planetary orbits

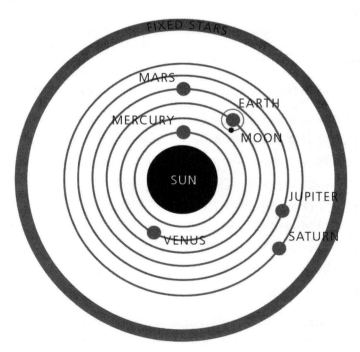

3.3.1 Implications of the heliocentric model

With Copernicus's new heliocentric paradigm, the changing motions and luminosity of the planets – as viewed from the earth – were just artefacts of the earth's motion. The unchanging arrangement of the stars was now due to their vast distance from our solar system. After Copernicus, the universe was no longer a spherical chamber constructed around mankind; instead mankind was just a speck in a potentially infinite universe. We are still struggling to adjust our egos to this new reality today.

Other little astronomical details were also suddenly more comprehensible. Solar and lunar eclipses, as well as the phases of the moon, became more intuitive. The slight difference between the apparent speed of the rotation of the sun and the stars became explicable. The sun appeared to move around the earth because the earth was turning on its axis every 24 hours; in addition, the earth was moving around the sun once, roughly, every 365 days. The earth's rotation around the sun meant that every year the stars appeared to complete one more revolution about the earth than did the sun. This meant that the stars' day was about 365/366 times as long as a solar day, or roughly 23 hours 56 minutes. (It takes a few minutes before this becomes intuitive!)

One of the classic features of scientific revolutions is their ability to make seemingly unrelated observations suddenly fit together and take on new significance. It is almost as if, prior to the revolution, scientists are staring at a confused jigsaw puzzle, unable to fit the pieces together. Once the paradigm shift occurs, the scientists see the picture they are trying to assemble – and suddenly it becomes possible to complete the jigsaw puzzle.

3.3.2 After Copernicus

Once Copernicus had straightened out the orbits of the planets and clarified how we look at the solar system, scientific progress picked up pace quite nicely. Tycho Brahe (1546–1601), a Danish nobleman, performed more precise measurements of the planetary orbits. Johannes

Kepler (1571–1630) used Brahe's data to deduce that the planets did not move in circles but instead followed ellipses. This allowed him to dispense with the second flawed axiom of astronomy. As a result he was able to derive mathematical laws describing planetary motion. Kepler's laws then inspired another scientific revolution when Isaac Newton (1642–1727) turned them into his universal law of gravity.

By comparison with the stagnation of the previous two millennia, the progression from Copernicus to Newton and the flowering of the modern scientific age moved at lightning speed. After Newton, the Copernican heliocentric system, with the earth moving in orbital motion, was firmly established as the dominant scientific paradigm. As far as scientists were concerned, Act V of the scientific revolution, the acceptance phase, was complete within about 100 years of Copernicus's death.

3.4 Bruno and Galileo

The Copernican revolution was not welcomed in all spheres. Despite some initial misgivings northern Europe came to embrace the new thinking and in time set itself on a path toward future progressive scientific revolutions. After 70 or so years southern Europe dug in its heals, with the Catholic Church choosing to suppress the scientific heliocentric theory. Northern Europe came to lead the subsequent scientific and industrial revolutions while southern Europe fell behind, leaving a legacy which divides the continent to this day.

One of the easiest logical progressions from Copernicus's theory goes something like this: if the sun is fixed and the stars are fixed, and the stars are very distant from the earth, then maybe the stars are just distant suns. If the stars are distant suns, and our earth rotates around our sun, then maybe there are other earths rotating around other suns. If so, it is very unlikely that our earth is at the centre of the universe: in fact there may be no centre of the universe. So maybe we are not so special after all. The Dominican friar Giordano Bruno (1548–1600) was unlucky enough to follow this line of reasoning thereby adding to an already long list of views which were, at that time, considered unacceptable by the Catholic Church. In 1600, after a seven year trial, he was burnt at the stake for heresy.

Galileo Galilei (1564–1642) was another early adopter of the Copernican theory. Galileo was lucky enough to have the benefit of the newly invented telescope. When Galileo turned his telescope on Jupiter he was able to see, for the first time, that Jupiter had a system of moons orbiting around it. Jupiter, together with its moons, was the closest thing possible to direct experimental proof of Copernicus's planetary theory. It was in effect a miniature copy of the solar system. As a result, Galileo began teaching the Copernican theory. He quickly got into trouble.

Initially the Catholic Church took a pragmatic line with Galileo. In effect he was told he could use the Copernican model as long as he did not teach that it was true. In essence he was told – use it, just don't believe it. Galileo more or less stuck to the letter of this 'don't preach what you practice' edict, but nevertheless made it abundantly clear that he really did believe the Copernican theory. This eventually led him to also be tried for heresy. Under threat of some re-educational torture, Galileo was persuaded to correct his thinking and was let off with a life sentence of house arrest.

The case against Galileo was re-opened by Pope John Paul II in 1979 and in 1992 he was posthumously declared innocent. Fortunately the backlash against other scientific revolutions has been less brutal than that against the Copernican one. Nevertheless, as Kuhn noted, the reaction of those with vested interests in preserving the status quo is almost always one of criticism and rejection, irrespective of the merit of an idea.

If we take the 1992 event as the final acceptance of the Copernican paradigm, then the whole process of this particular scientific revolution – from the first observed empirical discrepancies to the final recognition of the new theory – took about 2,500 years to complete.

3.5 Copernicus's Achievement

Before moving onto William Harvey and his theory of circulatory blood flow, it is worth pondering what Copernicus did and what he did not do. Copernicus did not make any new astronomical observations of significance. His breakthrough did not rely on new mathematics or other astronomical techniques. He did not produce a more accurate astronomical model than the previous Ptolemaic system. He provided no experimental demonstration that his model was superior to the Ptolemaic system.[7]

All that Copernicus did was to describe the universe in a simpler, more logical way. Copernicus provided conceptual efficiency. His triumph was in the elegance of his model, which allowed subsequent workers to think more clearly.

---

[7] In 1851 the French physicist Léon Foucault used a giant pendulum (Foucault's pendulum – it was an experiment before it was a book) to show that the earth was indeed spinning on its axis as Copernicus had guessed.

4 BLOOD AND BACON

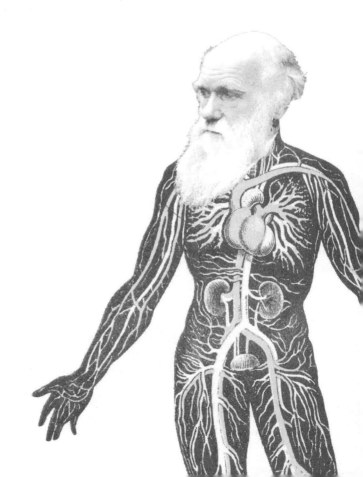

"Galen's anatomy and physiology were not in need of improvement, as Renaissance anatomists had attempted, but of complete rejection."

Andrew Gregory (Gregory, 2001)

WILLIAM HARVEY (1578–1657) was born 35 years after the death of Copernicus, and as a result would have grown up and been educated as the revolutionary Copernican theory was spreading throughout northern Europe. Like Copernicus he was the son of a wealthy family and was also able to study at the elite University of Padua, where he specialised in medicine and anatomy.

Harvey qualified as a physician in Padua, whereupon he returned to his native England and took up a position at St Bartholomew's hospital in London. Harvey was eventually to rise to become physician to King Charles I, who showed an active interest in his anatomical research. As court doctor, one of Harvey's patients was none other than the lord chancellor, Sir Francis Bacon, proponent of the Baconian scientific method. This connection between Bacon and Harvey was to lend fuel to an amusing conspiracy theory over the authorship of the plays of William Shakespeare, which emerged in Victorian times and is still running today (more on this later). Harvey's seminal work on human anatomy and the theory of blood flow through the body – *On the Motion of the Heart and Blood* – was published in 1628.

4.1 Hippocrates and his Theory of the Humours

Once again, to get the full story of Harvey's scientific revolution it is necessary to go back to the early Greek scholars.

When William Harvey studied medicine in Padua he would have been taught the theory of the bodily humours, an idea that could be traced back 2,000 years to the teachings of Hippocrates (460–370 BC). Even by the standards of ancient science, it was a daft theory. Hippocrates taught that the health of the body was controlled by the relative balance between four different bodily fluids known as the humours. These were: blood, phlegm, black bile and yellow bile. If these fluids were nicely balanced and in equilibrium then, according to the theory, the body would be healthy. If they were out of balance, in disequilibrium, then the body would be unhealthy.

With this idea of an ideal balance of the humours as a starting point, medical practice evolved along the lines of associating different ailments with different imbalances between the humours and then trying to find ways to restore the correct balance. This is likely the origin of the proverbial advice 'starve a fever and feed a cold', and is certainly behind the enthusiasm of medieval physicians for the practice of bloodletting.[8]

The theory of the humours became so dominant it was considered to be a self-evident truth that could not be challenged. In effect, it was the key axiom of medicine in Harvey's time.

4.1.1 Galen's theory of blood flow

At about the time that Ptolemy was tying astronomical thinking into pretzel-shaped knots by further confusing the ideas of Aristotle, Galen (129–200 AD) was doing the same thing with the ideas of Hippocrates. Galen claimed to have studied human anatomy and from this developed a theory of the movement of blood through the body.

In essence, Galen came to the conclusion that there were two related networks that transported blood through the body. These were the networks of the veins and the arteries. Galen believed each of these networks transported blood in the same way sap moves through a tree. In a tree, the flow starts from the roots, travels up through the trunk and then splits out into the branches, from where it moves through progressively smaller limbs until it reaches the leaves and then evaporates. In Galen's model, the roots of the blood system were in the liver where,

---

[8] Bloodletting is still practised today. It goes by the name of venesection, but it is used to correct abnormally high levels of iron in the blood rather than to rebalance the humours.

he believed, the blood was created from nourishment drawn from the stomach. From the liver, the blood then seeped slowly out through the larger veins, some being carried directly to the organs and some flowing to the right ventricle of the heart.

Once the blood reached the right ventricle of the heart it then passed through capillaries in the heart's muscular central wall, the septum, transiting into the left ventricle of the heart. Once in the left ventricle it was mixed with air that had been drawn from the lungs. This mixing with air, the 'concocting' process, changed the colour of the blood from deep red to bright red. The bright-red concocted blood then seeped out from the left ventricle through the arterial system to the rest of the body. Both the dark-red venous blood and the bright-red arterial blood were believed to evaporate, somehow, once they had reached the organs and extremities of the body.

In Galen's model the heart was recognised as a form of pump, but it was not a blood pump: it was a bellows, drawing air from the lungs.

From the perspective of ancient physicians, Galen's theory had much to commend it. He had explained why venous and arterial blood were different colours; he had offered a plausible story about the function and beating of the heart, which also appeared to fit its mechanical structure. Just as important, Galen's theory fitted nicely with Hippocrates's idea of equilibrium between the bodily humours. Like Ptolemy's version of astronomy, Galen's version of anatomy grew to dominate medicine for the next one and a half millennia.

4.1.2 Vesalius

In the early 16th century, at the same time Copernicus was unravelling the confusion of Ptolemaic astronomy, a Belgian anatomist and professor of Padua University, Andreas Vesalius (1514–1564), was trying to do the same with the work of Galen. In 1543, the same year in which Copernicus published his great work, Vesalius published his study of human anatomy, *On the Fabric of the Human Body*.

Vesalius's study contained so many corrections to Galen's version of anatomy that he concluded that Galen had actually studied pigs and monkeys rather than humans, as he claimed. For our purposes, however, Vesalius's most important finding was that there were no capillaries passing through the septum of the heart, and therefore blood could not move between the left and right ventricles of the heart as required by Galen's theory. Without these capillaries Galen's entire anatomical theory, which dominated all medical thinking at the time, was simply wrong.

At this point one would have expected a considerable amount of soul searching within the medical community followed by a burst of research activity as anatomists started looking for a better anatomical theory. In practice, this did not happen.

What actually happened was that the medical establishment carried on using Galen's theory and in subsequent editions of his work Vesalius was obliged to tone down his refutation of Galen's version of anatomy. This was a classic case of science operating as described by Kuhn – prevailing dogma triumphing over experimental data.

Vesalius had shown that Galen's model failed the empirical test. But as Kuhn explained, this was not enough for Galen's model to be rejected. Vesalius had not made the vital second step: he had not provided a better alternative theory. Until that happened, Galen's model remained the dominant paradigm.

This illustrates again one of the important suggestions of Kuhn's work. It appears that we humans cannot accept having no theory. We can be persuaded to step from one theory to another, better theory, but we cannot be persuaded to step from a wrong theory into the abyss while we wait for a better theory to come along. This is why, regardless of how many times the behaviour of the economy refutes current economic theory, that theory will not be rejected until a better model is proposed.

4.1.3 William Harvey's revolution

When William Harvey arrived to study medicine in Padua, half a century after Vesalius had published his findings, Galen's refuted theory still dominated the curriculum. Nevertheless Harvey's professors must have had their doubts as they had continued the research agenda pursued by Vesalius. Harvey's tutor, Hieronymus Fabricius (1537–1619), had made important discoveries concerning the development of the foetus and the function of the digestive tract. Fabricius had also found that larger veins contained valves, or "little doors" as he called them, though their purpose was unknown at the time.

Once back in London, Harvey continued the tradition of anatomical investigation he had learned in Padua. He conducted extensive anatomical research on humans and any other type of animal he could get hold of. He also became renowned for his public autopsies, performed over five days in a specially constructed demonstrating theatre. Weather permitting, the same cadaver was used in each of the five days.[9]

Harvey was an expert anatomist who studied the function of the heart and the circulatory system in considerable detail. He performed intricate, original and often gruesome experiments on both dead and live animals.[10] Despite this, possibly his most important experiment was also one of his simplest. By using a ligature to constrain the blood flow in the forearm of a patient, Harvey was able to show that blood flowed back through the veins from the extremities of the body towards its core – if the ligature was placed by the elbow then the blood backed up in the veins towards the fingers. This direction of flow, from periphery to core, was opposite to that required by Galen's theory. We cannot know for certain but it appears likely that reversing the direction of the flow of blood through the veins was the vital step allowing Harvey to reimagine the plumbing of the body.

[9] This may have been why Francis Bacon was so interested in preserving flesh with snow.

[10] Thomas Wright's *Circulation: William Harvey's Revolutionary Idea* (Wright, 2012) and Andrew Gregory's *Harvey's Heart: the Discovery of Blood Circulation* (Gregory, 2001) both give excellent accounts of Harvey's research.

With the direction of the blood flow in the veins reversed, Harvey was then able to understand that the venous system was not like a tree dispersing sap from roots, through trunk and branches to leaves; rather, it was like a river system collecting water through tiny streams, into larger tributaries and then into the main river. The venous system was not a blood-distribution system, it was a blood-collection system.

Once Harvey had reversed the direction of the flow of blood through the veins and understood the true function of the venous system, his circulatory theory was only a small step. He realised that the arteries were the distribution system for blood and the veins the collection system. He realised that blood flows around the body through a single continuous circuit between the bodily organs and the lungs, with one ventricle of the heart pumping blood from lungs to organs and the other from organs to lungs. The outward leg, from the lungs to organs, is pumped by the left ventricle, and the return leg from organs back to the lungs by the right ventricle.

Figure 7: A representation of Harvey's circulatory theory of blood flow

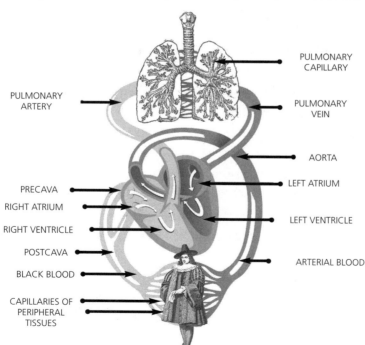

As with all of the best scientific revolutions, Harvey's new model was simpler than its predecessor and explained more. It was, for example, now clear why arteries had considerably thicker walls than veins – this was because they were on the downstream, high-pressure side of the heart. With Harvey's theory there was no need for the missing capillaries through the septum, or any complex concoction process.

4.2 Rejection and Acceptance

Harvey's new theory was not popular with his colleagues. For years, doctors had been making a healthy living bleeding their unhealthy patients dry. Harvey's circulatory theory challenged the wisdom of bloodletting and cast doubt on the whole notion of the theory of the bodily humours. Harvey's theory was not good for the vested interests of the medical profession and he was attacked accordingly. London's College of Physicians came out in favour of Galen's ideas and against Harvey's new theory.[11] A fellow physician, James Primrose, ridiculed Harvey's practice of experimenting with animals and criticised him for undermining the body of accepted wisdom.

Where Harvey had the upper hand, however, was that he could, through public demonstration, show the validity of his theory. Through these public demonstrations, Harvey's theory gained popular support and the medical profession reluctantly came into line. Harvey is one of the few scientific revolutionaries who saw his theory gain widespread popular support in his own lifetime.

4.3 Harvey, Bacon and the Shakespeare Controversy

The story of Harvey's discovery of the circulatory flow of blood is frequently cited as a near-perfect example of Francis Bacon's empirical

---

[11] Technically it was the Royal College of Physicians, though the label 'Royal' was not in common use at that time.

scientific method in action. As Bacon was a patient of Harvey, it is quite possible that the two men influenced one another. That said, Thomas Wright, one of Harvey's biographers, argues that closer study of Harvey's method suggests he did not follow Bacon's approach. Instead, Harvey arrived at the theory first and then constructed his experiments to confirm the theory and demonstrate its validity to others.

To quote Wright:

> "Harvey's most famous experiment was his measurement of the quantity of blood leaving the heart at the moment of contraction. In testing this, it has often been suggested that he proceeded along Baconian lines. After close observation, he devised the hypothesis that blood leaves the heart, in systole, and in considerable quantity. The next step was to establish how much blood was ejected with every contraction." (Wright, 2012)

If Wright is correct, then Harvey may have worked in the same way as Copernicus – idea first, confirmation later. Ironically, Harvey may have inspired Bacon's scientific philosophy while practising science quite differently.

While on the subject of the connection between Harvey and Bacon, it is worth taking a little time on the Victorian conspiracy theory over the authorship of the plays of William Shakespeare. The conspiracy theory involves both Harvey and Bacon and it goes along the following lines.

The plays of William Shakespeare are frightfully clever and demonstrate enormous learning. Therefore their author could not possibly be a commoner from a rural town like Stratford-upon-Avon. The true author must have been a learned gentleman of the highest standing.

The next step is to cast around for a suitable gentlemen who could have written the plays. Enter stage left – the lord chancellor, Francis Bacon; noted essayist, a very clever man and, importantly, a contemporary of Shakespeare. Therefore Francis Bacon was William Shakespeare.

All that's needed now is a little circumstantial evidence to support the theory, which is where William Harvey gets dragged into the plot.

Shakespeare died in 1616, 12 years before the 1628 publication of Harvey's circulatory theory of blood flow. However, Shakespeare's plays were not published until sometime after his death – and, crucially, after the publication of Harvey's theory. Therefore if the plays of Shakespeare contain reference to Harvey's theory, they must have been written after 1628 and *also* after Shakespeare's death. Better still, as Bacon was a patient of Harvey, Bacon would have been just the man to slip in a few oblique references to his doctor's work.

Enter stage right, Menenius from Shakespeare's *Coriolanus*. In the following passage, Menenius – who is speaking, rather oddly, from the perspective of the human stomach – seems to show clear knowledge of how blood flows through the body.

> That I receive the general food at first
> Which you do live upon; and fit it is,
> Because I am the storehouse and the shop
> Of the whole body: but, if you do remember,
> I send it through the rivers of your blood,
> Even to the court, the heart, to the seat o' the brain;
> And, through the cranks and offices of man,
> The strongest nerves and small inferior veins.

Therefore, according to one Dr Orville W. Owen (1854–1924), the author of *Coriolanus* knew of Harvey's theory of blood flow. Therefore the plays of Shakespeare were written after Harvey's theory was published and therefore after Shakespeare's death. By this logic, Shakespeare could not have written his plays, which leaves Bacon as the best contender for their authorship. QED – Bacon was the real Shakespeare.

It's a great Dan Brown-style story. Unfortunately, it's quite obviously wrong.

If you are a modern medical doctor, as Orville W. Owen was, you would be well-trained in Harvey's theory. Given this prior knowledge you may read the above passage, note the reference to blood flow, and think of William Harvey.

On the other hand if, for some very odd reason, you happen to have studied both the long-defunct theory of Galen and Harvey's replacement version, then you get to a different answer. The passage from *Coriolanus* clearly describes blood flowing outward, transporting nutrients from the stomach to the organs via the veins. It is *a* theory of blood flow, but the direction of the flow is in agreement with Galen's much older theory – not with Harvey's newer theory. Read in this way, the passage become evidence not for but *against* Bacon's authorship of the plays of Shakespeare.

Once again, the message is: the paradigm you use determines the way you interpret the data. On balance, it's probably best to stick with the simplest, most elegant paradigm. Shakespeare's plays were written by Shakespeare.

5 DARWIN'S
THEORY OF SPECIES

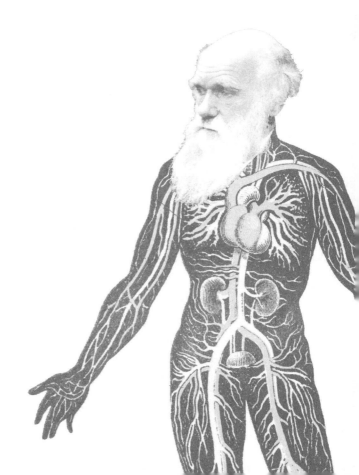

"No naturalist has devoted more painstaking attention to the structure of the barnacles than Mr Darwin."

Richard Owen (1804–1892)

CHARLES DARWIN (1809–1882) and Alfred Russel Wallace (1823–1913) are both credited as co-discoverers of the theory of evolution by natural selection. In what must be one of the more remarkable coincidences of science, Wallace set out his theory in a letter to Darwin in 1858. This prompted Darwin, who had been sitting on his own almost-identical theory for many years, to have both his and Wallace's ideas presented jointly that same year. A year later Darwin published his theory in full in his famous work *On the Origin of Species* (Darwin, 1859).

What is less well-known about the story of evolution is that Darwin and Wallace were just the last two in a long line of evolutionary theorists. By the time of the publication of *Origins*, evolution had been a controversy raging within Victorian society for decades.

5.1 Early Ideas of Species

The earliest theory of species and the one still dominant in Darwin's time was the biblical creationist theory. According to this idea, all species were created together with the earth and had remained unchanged ever since. This was a static-equilibrium theory, in which it was considered unthinkable that species could change form over time. The unchanging, immutable, nature of species was axiomatic to the understanding of biology prior to Darwin.

5.2 The Discrepancies

The creationist story began running into serious trouble toward the end of the 18th century, when disputes over the age of the earth began appearing.

In the 17th century, James Ussher (1581–1656), Archbishop of Armagh, had rather helpfully calculated the age of the earth through a mixture of biblical and historical research. According to Ussher, the earth was created on the night before Sunday 23 October 4004 BC. Quite how there was a night before Sunday 23 October 4004 BC is a bit of a mystery. Nevertheless, this made the earth about 6,000 years old, which at that time was taken to be the true age of the earth.

Fast forward a couple of hundred years into the late 18th and early 19th century and the idea of the earth being only 6,000 years old was starting to cause serious problems for the new science of geology. The eminent geologist, Sir Charles Lyell (1797–1875), thought the earth needed to be around 300 million years old.

The next problem for the creationist school was a growing body of evidence from the fossil record. Fossil-collecting had become a popular hobby, and taken as a whole the new fossil collections showed clear evidence that the earth had once been populated with many species – most dramatically, dinosaurs – that were no longer alive today. Equally puzzling was the fact that the fossil record showed a progression in the complexity of animals through time. The oldest fossil-bearing rocks contained evidence of only very simple fossils, while younger rocks contained much more complex fossils.

Aside from the fossil record, it had also been noted that mankind had already demonstrated the ability to alter species through the selective breeding of domesticated animals. Darwin himself confirmed these findings by selectively breeding pigeons at his country estate, Down House, just outside London.

The upshot of these observations was that, by the first half of the 19th century, long before Darwin published his theory, many people were already thoroughly convinced that an alternative to creationism was needed.

5.3 Alternative Theories of Species

Opinions were divided over how to tackle the problem of the fossil record. One group sought to reconcile the fossil record with creationism and another sought to replace creationism entirely.

The English naturalist, Philip Henry Gosse (1810–1888), came up with one of the more spectacularly silly ways of saving the creationist thesis. According to Gosse's book, *Omphalos*, which was published two years before Darwin's *Origins*, God had deliberately made the earth appear much older than it really was by creating an artificial fossil record. In essence, Gosse claimed the earth had been manufactured with an artificial patina of age, like a fake junk-shop antique. Even to Victorian England, this theory was too silly to be taken seriously.

Not to be outdone, Andrew Crosse, an English amateur scientist, came up with an equally creative idea. Crosse was one of the first scientists to study electricity and in 1836 he reported having observed live, fully-formed insects being spontaneously created by the electrical discharge in one of his experiments. This briefly led to the idea of the spontaneous generation of species through electrical discharge. Mercifully, the spark soon went out of this idea also.

More sensible evolutionary theories were also being proposed. The theory of *transformisme* or transmutation was proposed by the French naturalist Jean-Baptiste de Lamarck (1744–1829), who was the first to hit on the idea that species may adapt to their environment over multiple generations. Lamarck's suggestion was that animals acquire traits during their lifetime that help them survive better and then pass these on to their offspring.[12] Lamarck's idea explained why species may change but it did not explain why species should become more complex over time. For this, Lamarck had to assume some inherent underlying

---

[12] Lamarck's idea of inheritable acquired characteristics was strongly criticised at the time and discarded following Darwin's theory. Interestingly, however, the field of epigenetics has shown that the expression of certain genes can be influenced by environment and that in some cases these acquired traits can be passed on to offspring. So in a limited way at least Lamarck's idea appears to be valid.

complexifying force. As a result Lamarck's combined theory lacked both elegance and a convincing mechanism to explain increasing complexity; it did not gain traction.

In 1844, the idea of the transmutation of species entered the popular consciousness with the publication of *Vestiges of the Natural History of Creation* (Chambers, 1844) which, despite being widely criticised at the time, was an important attempt to link many of the emerging branches of science together into one coherent narrative. It became a worldwide best seller.

Vestiges discussed an array of competing evolutionary theories, including one apparently inspired by the work of the early computing pioneer, Charles Babbage. This theory suggested that species may be pre-programmed to transmute into new species after a certain number of reproductive cycles. This novel idea came from an iterative algorithm, demonstrated by Babbage, which produced sequential integers from 0 to 1,000,001 and then suddenly at the next iteration produced the number 100,010,002. The appeal of this theory was its ability to accommodate evolution and creationism. Still other theories were proposed, relating the transmutation of species to the gestation time of the foetus or to the environmental conditions experienced by the parents.

This proliferation of competing incompatible evolutionary theories before the emergence of Darwin's idea is another classic example of a field in a pre-revolutionary scientific crisis. The empirical evidence had showed the inadequacy of the old creationist paradigm. However, in the absence of a viable replacement theory, the majority clung, with varying degrees of enthusiasm, to the old creationist paradigm, while the minority cast about in chaotic search for better models.

5.4 Darwin's Breakthrough

Darwin succeeded where others had failed because he recognised the possibility of explaining both the transmutation of species and their increasing complexity with a single simple process. Despite the popular narrative, which focuses on Darwin's botanical research, his research was not the source of his breakthrough. Both of the novel ideas that Darwin drew upon to make his breakthrough came from the field of economics. (Chapter 8 returns this compliment by putting Darwin's idea back into economics.)

Robert Malthus (1766–1834) had published a controversial analysis of demographics in 1798, *An Essay on the Principle of Population*. Malthus had arrived at a bleak assessment of the prospects for mankind. He observed that due to our tendency to have large numbers of children, the human population tended to increase geometrically over time. Since the resources of the earth were limited, this geometric growth of population meant that mankind was fated to breed its way into poverty and starvation:

> "The power of population is so superior to the power of the earth to produce subsistence for man, that premature death must in some shape or other visit the human race."

The second idea borrowed from economics was the division of labour, this being the recognition that workers could improve their productivity through specialisation. This was one of Adam Smith's (1723–1790) great insights in *The Wealth of Nations*, published in 1776.

Darwin recognised the grim logic of Malthus's geometric growth rate of population meant that a large proportion of each generation of a species must die without reproducing. Therefore, he deduced, there must be competition between members of the same species for resources. And therefore this competition must mean that only the strongest, best adapted, of the species will survive to produce the next generation. His next step was to recognise that, since specialisation brought productivity gains, there would be a competitive benefit for species to become more specialised and therefore more complex over time. The pressure to survive produced both the force of adaptation and development at the same time. This is what we know today as evolution by natural selection.

The tendency of populations to grow geometrically meant that the competition within species was central to the Darwinian mechanism. When this idea was translated into its implications for mankind, there was no escaping that Darwinian evolution set man against man in an endless competitive fight for survival. Only people who outcompeted their neighbours would successfully pass on their characteristics to the next generation. To the Victorian sense of morality, this profoundly amoral theory was a tough pill to swallow.

5.5 The Rejection

Having dispensed with the need for an intelligent designer and turned nature into a brutal fight to the death, a religious backlash was to be expected. What was more interesting was the nature of the backlash from within the scientific community. The story can be told with reference to just one especially scathing review of *Origins* published anonymously in the *Edinburgh Review*. Shortly after publication it was revealed that the author was the, by then former friend of Darwin, eminent naturalist Richard Owen.

Owen's review was a spectacularly shoddy hatchet job. He went to great lengths to talk up his own work while belittling Darwin's contribution to the field. What is most interesting is how he chose to attack Darwin.

Owen reviews a long list of irrelevant details from Darwin's book, ranging from the anatomy of barnacles and the behaviour of ants, to a discussion of how bees make hexagonal honeycombs. Then he observes:

> "These are the most important original observations, recorded in the [*Origins of Species*]: they are, in our estimation, its real gems – few indeed and far apart, and leaving the determination of the origin of species very nearly where the author found it..."

> "...The scientific world has looked forward with great interest to the facts which Mr Darwin might finally deem adequate to the support of his theory on this supreme question in biology, and to

the course of inductive original research which might issue in throwing light on 'that mystery of mysteries.' But having now cited the chief, if not the whole, of the original observations adduced by its author in the volume now before us, our disappointment may be conceived."

What had really irked Owen was that, in his opinion, Darwin had made no important original observations. What is perhaps more surprising is that Owen was absolutely right. But Owen had entirely missed the point.

Darwin's theory was not about new observations. Like Copernicus's theory three centuries before him, Darwin's breakthrough relied on reinterpretation of existing knowledge. To Owen, who had spent a lifetime collecting and analysing new specimens, and who had expected this work to bring new insight, it was too much to take. He then went on to argue that somehow such theorising was not the job of real scientists:

> "The great names to which the steady inductive advance of zoology has been due during those periods, have kept aloof from any hypothesis on the origin of species."

Owen's message was: work harder, not smarter!

Owen then quotes himself, arguing that scientific progress is only allowable if it is made deductively:

> "Owen has long stated his belief that some pre-ordained law or secondary cause is operative in bringing about the change; but our knowledge of such law, if such exists, can only be acquired on the prescribed terms. We, therefore, regard the painstaking and minute comparisons by Cuvier of the osteological and every other character that could be tested in the mummified ibis, cat, or crocodile, with those of the species living in his time; and the equally philosophical investigations of the polypes operating at an interval of 30,000 years in the building up of coral reefs, by the profound paleontologist of Neuchatel, as of far higher value in reference to the inductive determination of the question of the

origin of species than the speculations of Demaillet, Buffon, Lamarck, *Vestiges*, Baden Powell, or Darwin."

Finally, and rather desperately, he tries to define what Darwin did as being outside of the realm of science: "classification is the task of science, but species the work of nature."

Owen's rationale for rejecting Darwin is a textbook response from the leader of a school of science that has just been overturned.

Finally, Owen, the leader of the old guard, bemoans the younger generation of naturalists leaving his sinking ship: "Thus several, and perhaps the majority, of our younger naturalists have been seduced into the acceptance of the homoeopathic form of the transmutative hypothesis now presented to them by Mr Darwin, under the phrase of 'natural selection'."

Owen was a logical Mr Spock faced with a problem that only an intuitive Captain Kirk could really solve. But enough of him. We'll leave this chapter with Darwin emphasising a point that will be picked up in later chapters.

> "Hence, as more individuals are produced than can possibly survive, there must in every case be a struggle for existence, either one individual with another of the same species, or with the individuals of distinct species, or with the physical conditions of life."
> (Darwin, 1859)

6 CONTINENTS
AND REVOLUTIONS

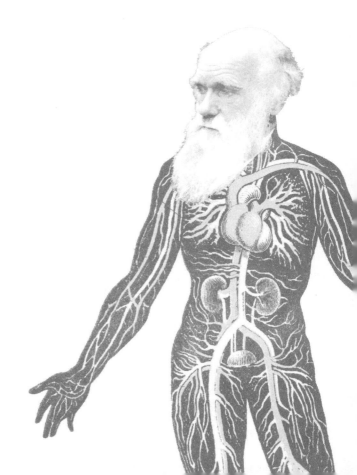

"In the 1950s it was claimed that a US geology lecturer could be dismissed for teaching Wegener."

Robert Muir Wood (Wood, 1985)

Darwin's theory of evolution was an interdisciplinary revolution. He used ideas from economics to solve a problem in biology that had been identified by paleontology. His theory of evolution then immediately helped cause a crisis in geology.

By the end of the 19th century, geology was the next of the big scientific disciplines to move into full-blown crisis. Darwin's new theory of evolution was causing problems for geologists, both through the fossil record and the evidence of living species. Darwin's theory meant that the probability of identical species evolving in geographically disconnected areas was so small as to be a practical impossibility. This left everyone scratching their heads trying to explain why the fossil record showed a commonality between, for example, South American and African dinosaurs.

Similar anomalies were identified with modern species: for example, the wildlife of Madagascar was found to be related to the wildlife on the distant landmass of Southern India, not that of the much closer continent of Africa. Somehow dinosaurs had travelled between South America and Africa and lemurs had travelled between Madagascar and India. Nineteenth-century geology could not explain how those journeys were possible.

The next of geology's problems was the inability to explain how mountains were made. In fact, geologists could not explain any example of folded rock strata, and that covers a big section of what geology is about. By this time things had moved on from the creationist theory of earth formation. The new idea was that the earth had formed from a giant cloud of gas. This gas had condensed into a hot ball of molten lava and that ball of lava had cooled into a solid ball of rock. According to this model the earth should be solid and perfectly smooth, like a giant marble – mountain ranges and continents were a problem.

Then there was the jigsaw puzzle problem. Ever since cartographers started producing accurate maps of the world, people had noticed that the west coast of Africa appeared to fit nicely into the east coast of South America as if they were pieces of a jigsaw puzzle. As the maps became better, it was realised that essentially all of the larger land masses of the earth could be rearranged, like the pieces of a jigsaw puzzle, into a single continent. When the underlying geological features on the continents of Africa and South America were also found to match up, the puzzle became impossible to dismiss as a coincidence. As physicist Alfred Wegener put it: "the map of the continents was as if they were all torn from a single sheet of newspaper. When correctly rearranged not only did their edges fit but so did the lines of text running across them."

Finally, there was the problem of gravity. At the start of the 20th century, the British government decided to perform a detailed survey of India. In the absence of satellite-based global positioning systems, this involved a painstaking process of triangulating the entire continent with the use of theodolites, surveying instruments that measure vertical and horizontal angles with a rotating telescope. A surveying task on this scale had never been attempted before and the surveyors soon ran into an unexpected problem. Their measurements were taken with reference to plumb lines, which were assumed to hang vertically, pointing toward the centre of the earth. However, it quickly became apparent that in certain locations the plumb lines did not hang exactly vertically; they were being pulled to the side by the gravitational effect of local geographical features.

When the surveyors were in northern India, the lines were being influenced by the gravitational pull of the Himalayan mountains; and, when close to the coast, by the difference in density between the rock of the continental shelf and the water of the ocean. To correct for these distortions it was necessary to estimate the gravitational pull of the mountains and the oceans relative to the continental planes. In effect, the surveyors had to weigh the oceans and the mountains.

To everyone's surprise, when the results of these gravitational calculations came in, the continental planes were found to be too light relative to the oceans, and the mountains too light relative to the planes. The Himalayan mountains did not weigh enough and the oceans weighed too much.

6.1 A Profusion of Explanations

What emerged from all of these different anomalous observations was a fascinating example of scientific crisis,[13] one that I believe has close parallels with what is going on in the field of economics today. The global community of geologists, physicists and earth scientists fractured into multiple schools of thought. Each school specialised in explaining one of the anomalies. Theories were developed that looked reasonable in isolation but could not be knitted together into a coherent theory of the earth.

6.1.1 Mountain formation

Two popular explanations of mountain formation evolved. I shall call these the shrivelling apple model and the cooling custard model.

According to the shrivelling apple model, the earth started as a hot ball of lava, which cooled from the outside in. A thin solid crust formed as an outer shell over the inner molten core of the earth. As the inner core continued to cool, it shrank due to thermal contraction. This left the outer shell oversized, and the shell collapsed inward, folding and rippling as it did so. The whole process is akin to the way wrinkles form on the surface of a shrivelling apple as it dries out.

The appeal of the shrivelling apple idea was its ability to explain the formation of mountains and continental plates. It was also argued that it could permit land bridges to form and then vanish between the continents, thereby explaining how animal species had been able to move between disconnected continents (this was known as the land-bridge theory).

---

[13] Detailed accounts of this scientific crisis are given in Naomi Oreskes's *The Rejection of Continental Drift* (Oreskes, 1999) and Robert Wood's *The Dark Side of the Earth* (Wood, 1985).

The cooling custard model was a little different. According to this idea, as the earth cooled, patches of the earth's surface solidified into solid rock, while other areas remained molten. These solid areas then formed the continental plates. As the remaining molten earth continued to cool it contracted, pulling the ocean areas down, leaving the continents standing proud. In this model, mountains were supposedly caused by a twisting force on the earth's crust as the ocean floors fell relative to the continents. Apparently this model was popular in America, where the mountains tended to be close to the edge of the continents (at least if you ignore the ones that are very obviously not!). It was less popular in Europe and Asia, as their mountains are in the middle of the continents.

Frankly, neither model provided a convincing explanation of mountain formation, let alone how complex rock-folds occur. What's more, they said nothing very useful about any of the other big anomalies dogging geology like the jigsaw puzzle or the fossil record. Despite this, these models garnered impassioned support.

6.1.2 Balloon theory

Another set of theories emerged that were aimed at addressing the jigsaw puzzle problem. These focused on the idea that the earth was expanding rather than contracting. The idea was that the continents had originally formed a crust over the entire surface of a much smaller earth. When this earth subsequently expanded like a balloon, the crust was torn apart along fracture lines, splitting the once-complete crust into today's modern continents. New areas of thinner crust were formed, like scar tissue, in between the continents; and these became the oceans.

This model provided a very plausible explanation of the jigsaw puzzle problem. However, it was quite incompatible with mountain formation: inflating balloons don't spontaneously grow mountains. What's more, there was no plausible explanation for the earth growing in this way. Matter accretion, the idea that the atoms of the earth were spontaneously multiplying, was considered, as was the idea that gravity might be getting weaker, allowing the earth to expand. Neither seemed very likely.

Aside from this, both of these ideas required the rewriting of large areas of physics. Since it was not thought wise to throw a good science under the bus in order to save a failing science, the balloon theory was soon deflated. This left the jigsaw puzzle as a glaring anomaly, with no credible explanation. For the most part, geologists dealt with the jigsaw puzzle of the continents by ignoring it almost entirely.

6.1.3 Iceberg theory

Another group sought to explain the strange gravitational anomalies thrown up by the survey of India and by later surveys of America. The best contender was the idea of isostasy. This theory suggested that the continents were areas of solid rock floating on a substrate of denser molten rock. In essence, the idea was that the continents were akin to floating icebergs. The greater the volume of ice above the water, the greater the volume of ice needed below the water to provide buoyancy. This theory explained why the highest mountains like the Himalayas would be especially short of gravity, relative to their size.

Isostasy ran into vigorous opposition from geophysicists who insisted that the earth was so old by now that it must have already cooled into a solid ball of rock, in which case there could not possibly be a molten substrate beneath the crust. Surprisingly, most geologists accepted the solid-earth theory, despite the very obvious evidence of liquid rock bubbling up to the surface in and around volcanos. Since the presence of molten rock could not be explained by the prevailing paradigm, it was simply ignored. Once again, a pattern of disregarding experimental evidence if it conflicted with the favoured story was repeated.

6.1.4 Continental drift

In 1912, Alfred Wegener (1880–1930) came up with the brilliant solution that resolved all of the major problems of geology in one simple theory. Wegener was a highly respected German atmospheric physicist. He was therefore almost a complete outsider to the club of professional geologists. His brilliant idea – continental drift – took the best bits from all of the competing schools of geological thought and combined them together into one elegant coherent model that resolved all of the major anomalies of the field.

The continents, Wegener said, were indeed floating on a bed of molten rock according to the theory of isostasy. They had originally been connected in one super continent that had broken apart into today's smaller continents. These were now drifting across the globe and occasionally crashing into one another, creating mountain ranges and rock folds when they did so. Wegener's model had it all explained: mountain formation, the jigsaw puzzle problem, the fossil record, gravitational anomalies and even the lemurs of Madagascar – Madagascar was found to have originally been attached to southern India.

You might have thought that geologists would have been delighted that Wegener had fixed their science. Sadly, it did not play out that way. The vested interests circled the wagons and set out to protect their pet theories. Most, though not all, of the geological community rejected Wegener's idea.

The criticism thrown at Wegener was strikingly similar to that levelled at Darwin. The esteemed British physicist, Lord Kelvin, fought hard to defend his own idea that the earth was made of solid rock. The eminent American geologist, Harry Fielding Reid, reviewed the theory of continental drift in 1922, giving Wegener the same dismissive treatment that Owen had doled out to Darwin:

> "There have been many attempts to deduce the characteristics of the earth from a hypothesis; but they have all failed…This is another of the same type. Science has developed by the painstaking comparison of observations and, through close induction, not by first guessing at the cause and then deducing the phenomena."

Note the similarity of Reid's criticism of Wegener to that of Owen's criticism of Darwin. Both men resisted the idea that science could progress through intuitive leaps, insisting that progress was only permissible if it resulted from making ever more measurements. Reid, like Owen, was again demanding: work harder like Spock, not smarter like Kirk.

One of the most interesting aspects of the whole story of continental drift is the inability of scientists to believe that the earth's core was molten, despite the spectacularly obvious evidence of volcanic and seismic activity. Kuhn's analysis suggests that this is because they did not have a story to describe how it could still be molten. Without a good story, they simply ignored the implications of the flowing lava!

Shortly after Wegener published his idea of continental drift it was realised that radioactive decay, which had been recently discovered by the husband-and-wife team of Pierre and Marie Curie, generated heat and this heat was sufficient to keep the earth's core molten. Once the idea of radiogenic heat became accepted, the idea of a molten core beneath the earth's crust also started gaining support. Then it was realised that a hot fluid core must have convection currents within it that could act as the driving force to move the continents. Just as Kuhn's analysis suggested, geologists were only able to accept the reality of the earth's molten core once they had a story – radiogenic heat – to explain it. Without the explanatory story, the experimental evidence of molten lava was not enough to make geologists doubt the solid-earth model.

Even with the core now liquefied, a clear driving force for continental drift identified and a whole raft of supportive empirical evidence, large groups of geologists still held out against Wegener's idea until the 1960s. Just as Kuhn explained, new theories rarely change old minds. Wegener's brilliantly simple, clearly superior paradigm, had to wait for the old guard to fade away before becoming fully accepted.

6.2 Lessons of the Revolutions

For any readers who have stuck with me through the entrée of Kuhn, Copernicus, Harvey, Darwin and Wegener – thank you. It is now almost time to move to the main course, the scientific crisis currently bedevilling economics, and from there on to the dessert: a suggested path out of this crisis.

But before moving on, I must confess to a scientifically inexcusable selection bias. The four scientific revolutions I have discussed so far are not a random selection of all such revolutions. The stories I have told have been selected because they share some common features that I believe are relevant to both the crisis within economics and its potential resolution.

All four stories show that scientific progress was held back by dogmatic adherence to a static, equilibrium-centred, paradigm: astronomy had its stationary earth, medicine its equilibrium of the humours, biology its immutable species, and geology its solid earth with immovable continents. In all cases, the path to scientific progress required overturning the equilibrium paradigm and moving to a dynamic, usually circulatory, paradigm. Copernicus made the earth circulate around the sun. Harvey made blood circulate around the body. Darwin made species evolve and Wegener made continents move, pushed by circulating currents within the earth's core.

Today's dominant school of economics is also a static equilibrium paradigm. The rest of this book is an argument for rejecting the static equilibrium paradigm of economic theory and adopting in its place a circulatory paradigm.

PART II ECONOMICS

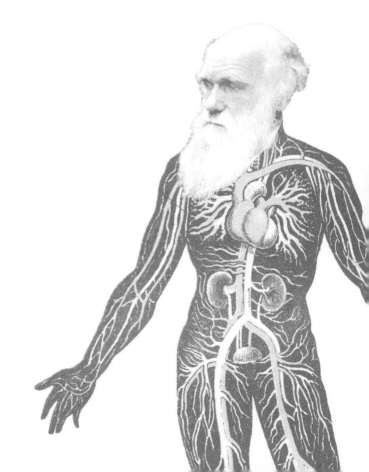

7 ECONOMICS –
RIPE FOR REVOLUTION

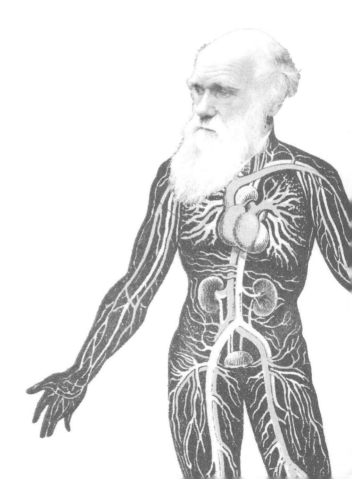

"As in manufacture, so in science – retooling is an extravagance to be reserved for the occasion that demands it. The significance of crises is the indication they provide that an occasion for retooling has arrived."

Thomas Kuhn

IN 1999 EDWARD LAZEAR, the former chief economic advisor to President George W. Bush, wrote a paper with the intriguing title of 'Economic Imperialism' (Lazear, 2000). Lazear begins his paper with the following bold claims:

> "Economics is not only a social science, it is a genuine science. Like the physical sciences, economics uses a methodology that produces refutable implications and tests these implications using solid statistical techniques. In particular, economics stresses three factors that distinguish it from other social sciences. Economists use the construct of rational individuals who engage in maximising behaviour. Economic models adhere strictly to the importance of equilibrium as part of any theory."

Lazear's paper is well worth taking the time to read as it is an elegant description of today's dominant neoclassical school of economics. But is it correct to assert that economics has achieved the status of being a genuine science? Some economists may believe they have graduated to the science faculty, but popular humour suggests the world at large thinks otherwise:

Economics is the only subject where the exam questions remain the same each year.

It's the answers that keep changing.

The purpose of this chapter is to argue that, to an objective observer looking in at the field of economics from outside, economics today exhibits all of the symptoms of being in one of Thomas Kuhn's states of pre-revolutionary scientific crisis. If this is a correct diagnosis, then the bad news is that economics has not yet become a real science. However, the good news is that there is hope that there may be a paradigm shift out there that is able to put economics on a path to becoming a proper science.

The symptoms suggesting economics is in a state of crisis are broadly as follows:

1. Economics has fractured into too many incompatible schools of thought to be considered a single science. In this respect it is analogous to astronomy prior to Copernicus, biology prior to Darwin and geology prior to Wegener.

2. The debate between the various schools of economics has broken down. Their various paradigms have become incommensurable, such that they cannot recognise when opposing schools hold valid positions. There are fundamental differences of opinion over the appropriate realm of economics and its methodology.

3. The mathematical models used by economists are proliferating and their complexity growing. Despite this, their predictive ability is not obviously improving.

4. Many of the important schools of economics operate unscientifically in that they do not attempt to model the real economy, but rather advocate reforming the real economy to conform to their own models.

5. The dominant neoclassical school of economics is built upon axioms that have been refuted by other fields. Meanwhile most of the alternative, heterodox schools also rest on logically flawed arguments.

6. The economics profession itself shows considerable inconsistency over time. The various schools of thought move in and out of fashion depending on the prevailing economic weather conditions in a most unscientific way.

7. Finally, important economic questions go unanswered and in some important areas even unasked. There is an unscientific tendency to ignore difficult questions that do not fit the paradigm.

7.1 Economics in a State of Un-civil War

My initial intention with this chapter was to look for generally agreed definitions of what each school of economics believes and then use these definitions as a starting point to compare and contrast them. However, in searching for the definitions, I rapidly reached the conclusion that economics has developed something akin to a fractal structure. By this I mean that the positions held by the different schools of economic thought have become like a coastline; no matter how closely you look at them, you never get to a resolution powerful enough to say that their position is well-defined and generally accepted. Instead you find only layer upon layer of ever-finer subdivisions and disagreements.

This fragmented fractal structure provides economics as a whole with a formidable defensive mechanism. It becomes almost impossible to survey and discuss even a narrow section of the field without becoming entangled in detailed disputed definitions. If you cannot even define what you're discussing, it becomes fiendishly difficult to mount any effective critique of the field.

In order to try to cut through this problem of information overload I have decided to take the proverbial 60,000-ft perspective, limiting the discussion to just the most widely recognised schools of thought, these being the schools of economics going by the names of: classical, neoclassical, libertarian, monetarist, Keynesian, Austrian, Marxist, institutional, and finally the behavioural school.

At this level of resolution there is at least a degree of agreement that each of these schools exists and represents a distinct subdivision of economics. However, the problem of defining what each of these subdivisions actually means remains tricky. In the absence of a better solution, I have simply chosen to give my own personal definitions of each school. I expect that almost every reader will disagree with some element of how I have characterised, or perhaps caricatured, each school. I hope these inevitable definitional disagreements do not obscure the real point of this chapter, which is to highlight that there are material divisions and inconsistencies between the different schools of economics today. It is the existence of these divisions and inconsistencies that provides the evidence for economics being in crisis, rather than the definitions of the schools themselves.

Before delving into the discussions of each of the schools, it is necessary to make a further point. John Maynard Keynes made an interesting observation on the difficulties involved in forecasting financial markets. Keynes likened market forecasting to trying to predict the outcome of a beauty contest. The problem is, he said, not one of identifying the most beautiful woman, but rather one of identifying the woman that the judges consider to be the most beautiful. This beauty contest observation has an analogue for economists like Keynes himself and their theories. In economics it is not important what the great economists actually said, what matters is what their followers today believe that they said.

I say this upfront, because the big schools of economic thought are all defined by an association with one or more of the big economists of history. Often when you look at the ideas promoted by the different schools today the messages are no more than unequivocal caricatures, or simplistic heuristics, of the more nuanced positions of their original figureheads. This leads to a second problem in defining the schools: when discussing, for example, Keynesianism, should we talk about what Keynes actually said or what today's Keynesians say? I've opted for the latter, as it is today's reinterpretation that is driving current policymaking.

So I shall be discussing the modern expressionist versions of the old masterpieces.

7.1.1 The classical and neoclassical schools of economics

The Scottish philosopher Adam Smith is widely considered to be the father of modern economics. Smith set out the core tenants of what was to become known as classical economics in his masterpiece *The Wealth of Nations*, published in 1776. Almost two and a half centuries later, the dominant school of economics, neoclassical economics, still considers itself to be based on Smith's work.

The following passage from the Nobel laureate George Stigler (1911–1991) helps give a flavour of what the neoclassical school has taken from Smith:

> "Smith had one overwhelmingly important triumph: he put into the centre of economics the systematic analysis of the behaviour of *individuals pursuing their self-interest* under conditions of *competition*. This theory was the crown jewel of *The Wealth of Nations*, and it became, and remains to this day, the foundation of the theory of the allocation of resources. The proposition that resources seek their most profitable uses, so that in *equilibrium* the rates of return to a resource in various uses will be equal, is still the most important substantive proposition in all of economics.

> "His construct of the *self-interest-seeking* individual in a *competitive* environment is *Newtonian* in its universality. That we are today busily extending this construct into areas of economic and social behaviour to which Smith himself gave only unsystematic study is tribute to both the grandeur and durability of his achievement." [Emphasis added] (Stigler, 1976)

This passage contains the key defining ideas of classical economics. Individuals act in their own self-interest, in competition with one another, producing a system that is in equilibrium. And that these are universal truths for economics in the way that Newton's laws are for physics.

More recently, Alan Greenspan, the former chairman of the US Federal Reserve Bank, gave a memorial lecture about Adam Smith, making the following points:

> "Perhaps if *The Wealth of Nations* had never been written, the Industrial Revolution would still have proceeded into the 19th century at an impressive pace. But without Smith's demonstration of the *inherent stability* and *growth* of what we now term *free-market* capitalism, the remarkable advance of material well-being for whole nations might well have been quashed. Pressures conceivably could have emerged to strengthen mercantilistic regulations in response to the stresses created by competition and

to the all-too-evident ills of industrialisation ...one could hardly imagine that today's awesome array of international transactions would produce the relative economic *stability* that we experience daily if they were not led by some international version of Smith's invisible hand." [Emphasis added] (Greenspan, 2005)

Greenspan emphasises the importance of free markets and deregulation. Again, the concept of stability is central to the interpretation. Greenspan goes as far as saying that Smith demonstrated the inherent stability of free-market capitalism.

I think it is uncontroversial to state that the core idea of the classical school of economics is that if individuals are permitted to pursue their own self-interest, in a competitive free-market system, the economy will achieve a condition of optimal equilibrium, which maximises the collective welfare of society at large. The notion that the force of competitive self-interest inadvertently acts in the best interest of society as a whole is what is meant by Smith's famous invisible hand:

"Every individual is continually exerting himself to find out the most advantageous employment for whatever capital he can command. It is his own advantage, indeed, and not that of the society which he has in view. But the study of his own advantage naturally, or rather necessarily, leads him to prefer that employment which is most advantageous to society...He intends only his own gain, and he is in this, as in many other cases, led by an invisible hand to promote an end which was not part of his intention." (Smith, 1776)

This leads to a basic philosophy of the classical school of economics that advocates a society in which individuals are, as far as is practicable, left alone to act in their own self-interest. Any government interference with economic activity is seen as an impediment to the ideal free-market system and should be minimised or eliminated. The classical school of economics is therefore a theory of the private sector of the economy only. In classical economics, the government sector is either ignored completely or treated as a regrettable distortion.

Turning classical economics into neoclassical economics has essentially been an exercise in first turning Smith's ideas into a set of mathematical axioms and then using those axioms to derive mathematical models to describe the economy. Implicit in this approach is the assumption that, as Stigler asserted, Smith's construction represented a truth that is *Newtonian in its universality*. In other words, neoclassical economists believe they are involved in a scientific quest to discover universal mathematical models that describe how the economy works in the same way that physicists pursue laws to describe natural phenomenon. The neoclassical project has been an exercise in making Smith's insight look as much like Newtonian physics as possible.

The economists Christian Arnsperger and Yanis Varoufakis have done an excellent job of distilling neoclassical economics down to its three core axioms in their recent paper *What is Neoclassical Economics?* (Arnsperger et al., 2006). Their language is a little more precise than mine, but for our purposes I think it is sufficient to describe these axioms as follows:

1. Individualism: people make their decisions independently of one another based on their own self-interest.

2. Maximisation: the decisions made by individuals are always designed to maximise their own welfare.

3. Equilibrium: the result of all of these individual optimising decisions is a stable system in optimal equilibrium.

Many of the most important disputes within the field of economics can be thought of as arguments over these three axioms. Indeed I suspect that at least some neoclassical economists would dispute that the equilibrium condition is an axiom at all, and instead argue that it is the inevitable consequence of the first two axioms. This is certainly the inference of Alan Greenspan's comment – "Smith's demonstration of the *inherent stability* and *growth* of what we now term *free-market* capitalism" – which appears to suggest that Smith proved rather than assumed stability. Most neoclassical economists would, I suspect, choose to argue that the equilibrium condition was demonstrated not by Smith but by Léon

Walras in the 1870s. Nevertheless, whether it is an axiom or not, equilibrium remains at the very centre of the neoclassical paradigm.

Before discussing various challenges to the neoclassical school of economics, it is worth again emphasising the elephant in the room, or more accurately the elephant that is not in the room. The neoclassical school is a framework for understanding the behaviour of self-interested individuals. In a modern developed economy, roughly half of the economic activity is due to the government; but there is no government in the basic neoclassical framework. To the extent that government is incorporated into the neoclassical framework, it is treated as a distortion.

Without integrating government into its framework, the neoclassical school cannot be considered to be a complete scientific model of a modern economy. This is my first quibble with neoclassical economics as a science – it's like studying the anatomy of an arm through the analysis of the biceps, without paying attention to the triceps. Neoclassical economics is unscientific in that it disregards half of the economic system.

7.1.2 The Austrian school of economics

The Austrian school of economics is often incorrectly considered to be synonymous with the neoclassical school. In practice, these schools differ in a number of important ways. The most obvious dispute between the Austrians and the neoclassical school is associated with the idea of equilibrium. The neoclassical school believes the natural state of an economy is in equilibrium, and if pushed away from equilibrium it will return, under its own impetus, to equilibrium. By contrast, the Austrian school believes the economy naturally has a boom–bust cyclical character, meaning that the economy is always oscillating about an equilibrium.

According to the Austrian school, the boom–bust business cycles are caused by credit cycles. When economic conditions are strong, banks tend to lend money more freely, causing economic conditions to strengthen, causing yet more lending and so on. When economic conditions are weak, banks tend to restrict credit, causing weaker economic conditions, and even less lending and so on. It's not a difficult argument to grasp and it has an awful lot of compelling empirical evidence on its side, but it runs headlong into two of the three axioms of the neoclassical school. From the Austrian perspective, credit cycles act to synchronise the economic decisions of individuals such that they can no longer be considered independent. As a result, individuals cease to act as individuals and instead act as a herd, making collective decisions. These collective decisions are then large enough to undermine any natural tendency toward equilibrium, causing the cyclical behaviour.

The essence of the clash between the Austrian and neoclassical schools is therefore whether or not to model the actors within an economy as though they behave as herding animals (wildebeest, say), or as solitary animals (e.g. leopards). The large number of neoclassical economists have all agreed that they are individuals, while the much smaller number of Austrians think they are not. Think of the scene in the movie *Life of Brian* when the whole crowd declares at once "Yes, we are all individuals" followed by the loan voice protesting "I'm not". The neoclassical crowd are the ones shouting in unison, "Yes, we are all individuals", while the lone Austrian is replying "I'm not".

This difference of opinion over individualism leads to a stark difference of judgement between the Austrian and neoclassical schools over policy recommendations and the correct methodology of economics. Austrians tend to advocate linking the currency of an economy to gold or otherwise reforming the monetary system so as to curtail the banking system's ability to extend credit. These measures are designed to limit the potential amplitude of the destabilising credit cycles caused by the herding activity of banks and borrowers. By contrast, the neoclassical school does not recognise this phenomenon and says little or nothing about banking, credit or monetary systems.

Because Austrians believe that forces can act in an economy to synchronise decision-making, they also reject the idea that it is possible to mathematically model an economy based on a simplistic adding up of the decisions of individuals. As a result, the Austrian school tends to argue against mathematical models, seeing the mathematical models of the neoclassical school as dangerously naïve. By contrast, the neoclassical school tends to view the Austrians as mathematically illiterate, unscientific hand-wavers.

This difference in perspective on core principles and the basic working methodology of economics leads to a significant problem in establishing a productive dialogue between the neoclassical and Austrian schools. The two schools to some extent suffer Kuhn's incommensurability problem. For example, when an economy suffers a downturn, the Austrian school will attempt to understand it in terms of forces generated internally within the system, by the herding behaviour of individuals. Meanwhile the neoclassical economists will tend to look for external factors responsible for pushing the economy away from equilibrium.

Philosophically the Austrian school sees the business cycle as a necessary and healthy aspect of the economy, believing occasional waves of, what they call, creative destruction (recessions) are necessary in order to purge the system of weaker business and excess credit making room for more vibrant business to take their place. The neoclassical school has no framework for understanding business cycles and therefore tends to attribute any apparent cyclicality to government policy mistakes or external, exogenous shocks.

Where the Austrian and neoclassical schools are in complete agreement is in their shared position on the benefits of low taxation, light regulation and minimal government. For this reason the policy recommendations of the Austrian and neoclassical schools often look similar, hence to the outside observer the two schools can become confused. From a policy perspective, Austrian economics is the same as the neoclassical school with the additional recommendations of banking and monetary reform. While the advocacy of low tax and light regulation generally appeals to the business sector the banking and monetary reform is, at least to the banking industry, unattractive. For this reason neoclassical economics is generally more popular in the business community than Austrian economics.

As with the neoclassical school the Austrian school also makes no effort to integrate government into its core paradigm. Austrians also see the government as a distortion to a system that would function better without it, albeit in a cyclical manner. For this reason Austrian economics is also a model of only half of the modern economic system.

7.1.3 The libertarian school of economics

The libertarian school of economics shares its advocacy of small government, low taxation and light regulation with both the Austrian and neoclassical schools. Some advocates of libertarianism go to the logical extreme of arguing for no government, no taxation and no regulation, claiming that all of the functions of government can be better provided by privately organised or funded initiatives.

It is possible to arrive at this position through either the Austrian or neoclassical schools, and for this reason any two libertarians may share similar policy objectives but have quite divergent underlying economic paradigms.

I have called the libertarian movement a distinct school of economics, but it may be better thought of as an advocacy group, arguing for a smaller government sector, representing the interests of both the Austrian and neoclassical schools.

The economic plane

At this point I wish to introduce a simple method of classifying the various schools of economics. Traditionally economic ideas are considered on a simplistic left–right spectrum, with Marxism on the left and the neoclassical, Austrian and libertarian schools on the right. This one-dimensional classification system is unable to correctly express the important differences between many of the competing schools.

For this reason I shall use a two-axis system, to define a two-dimensional X-Y plane. The bottom X-axis describes the school's attitude to the notion of equilibrium. If the school is placed on the left it does not believe the economy and market system is a naturally stable equilibrating system, while on right the school does believe in equilibrium. The vertical Y-axis is then used to represent the school's attitude to government. Schools represented at the bottom of the chart advocate small government, low tax and light regulation while those at the top advocate larger governments, higher tax and stronger regulation.

This classification system allows us to differentiate between the three schools discussed so far. The neoclassical, Austrian and libertarian schools are spread out on the X-axis but clustered together on the Y-axis, as shown in figure 8.

Figure 8: The economic plane showing the Austrian, neoclassical and libertarian schools of economics

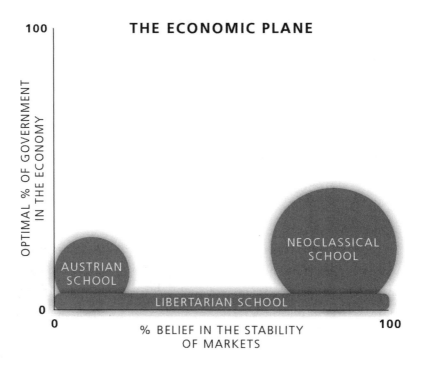

These three schools of economic thought share the common belief in the primacy of the pursuit of self-interest as the engine of economic activity.

They also share a disdain for large government. However, they disagree over individual action and the idea of equilibrium.

Maximisation vs competition

At this point I wish to make an observation about what is meant by the pursuit of self-interest. Economists frequently discuss the pursuit of self-interest as if it were a competitive process. However, economists do not model the pursuit of self-interest as a competitive process but as a maximising or optimising process. There is a subtle difference between these two processes.

If we were to boil it down to purely monetary terms, in the neoclassical maximisation world, entrepreneurs are all attempting to accumulate the maximum possible amount of money. In a competitive world, on the other hand, entrepreneurs are all attempting to accumulate more money than each other. In sporting terms it is the difference between one group of runners, all of whom are trying to run as fast as they possibly can, versus another group who are trying to run faster than each other. I shall leave this observation hanging for now, but its significance will become apparent in the next chapter.

7.1.4 Monetarist school

The monetarist school of economics[14] shares much of the analysis of the Austrian school but has a couple of important differences. Both the monetarists and the Austrians recognise an inherent cyclicality or instability in the economy and they both agree that its cause originates in the monetary and banking system. Where these schools differ is in what they think should be done about this instability.

---

[14] Note that I am using the term 'monetarist school' to cover all schools that advocate the management of money and credit in the economy, including via the manipulation of interest rates and quantitative easing. I am not confining the monetarist school to just monetarism of the type practised in the early 1980s under Margaret Thatcher. I consider this version of monetarism to be just one flavour of a much larger group of related strategies.

The Austrian school argues for reform of the banking and currency system so as to minimise the magnitude of the credit cycles, but otherwise argues to leave the economy alone to go through its natural boom-bust cycles. By contrast, the monetarist school argues that the cycles can and should be managed by controlling the amount of money in the economy. Controlling how much money is in the economy is, according to the monetarist school, the function of government.

Philosophically, the monetarist school's paradigm sits somewhere between the Austrian and neoclassical schools. The monetarists agree with the Austrians that the economy is unstable, but believe that it should be stabilised to look more like the economy that the neoclassical school would like to have. And the monetarists differ from both neoclassical and Austrian schools in that their school of thought does assign the government some role in the economy. Specifically, the monetarists believe it is the role of government, usually but not always via their central banks, to control and manage the overall activity of the private sector by manipulating various monetary instruments.

For this reason I have placed the monetarist school mid-way between the Austrian and neoclassical schools on the X-axis of our economic plane but a little higher on the Y-axis, reflecting the integration of government into the monetarist paradigm.

Figure 9: The economic plane with the addition of the monetarist school of economics

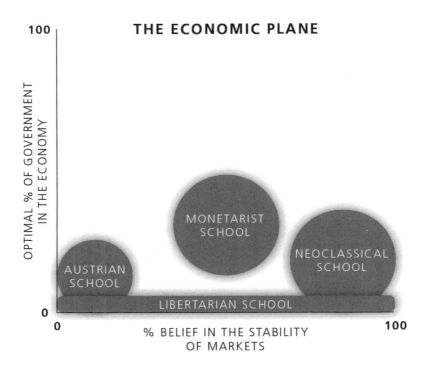

The monetarist school is one of the areas where the fractured fractal nature of economics becomes most pronounced. It is easy to advocate controlling the economy via its monetary system but less easy to specify how to do this. Does it mean controlling the amount of notes and coins in circulation (this was once believed to be a good idea) or does it mean controlling the amount of credit in the economy (this is the current approach)?

Then there is the question of what you should try to control. Governments have at times tried to control inflation, unemployment, economic activity, foreign exchange rates and interest rates with monetary methods. These choices give economists plenty of room to split into all sorts of monetarist faculties within the broader school. From a monetarist's perspective this is a wonderful state of affairs as there is always another approach that can be tried out when the last fad has failed – and it should be said there is a long and growing list of failures for this particular school.

In this book I generally refer to the neoclassical school of economics as the dominant or mainstream school of economics. This is probably still true in academic circles, but from an economic policy perspective the manipulation of the economy through monetary channels has gained such universal acceptance that the monetarist school is now overwhelmingly dominant. Since 2008 the enthusiasm for ever larger, more experimental, monetary policies has grown significantly.

For this reason the monetarist school should probably be considered the dominant paradigm for policy issues while the neoclassical school remains the dominant academic paradigm. Just as Galileo was put in the untenable position of being asked to practise Copernican astronomy while continuing to preach Ptolemaic astronomy, so many of today's leading economists, especially those staffing the central banks, preach neoclassicism whilst practising monetarism. This gap between theory and practice is another clear sign of economics being in crisis.

Given how important the monetarist schools have become, it is worth taking a little time to understand the origin of monetarism and then to consider a worrying philosophical challenge to the entire framework of the monetarist paradigm.

7.1.4.1 The historical origin of the modern monetarist school

Monetarism is often traced back to an essay written by David Hume in 1750, 'Of Money', though amusingly its birth date could be pushed back even earlier to 1526 when our old friend Copernicus wrote about minting coins.

Copernicus apparently described a version of Gresham's law (the idea that bad coins drive out good coins) and presented an early monetarist argument linking the price level to the amount of money in circulation. For our purposes, however, it is more informative to look at the more recent reincarnation of monetarism, which arose in 1933 with the publication by the American economist Irving Fisher of 'The Debt-Deflation Theory of Great Depressions'.

The following passages are taken from Fisher's paper:

> "Assuming, accordingly, that at some point of time, a state of over-indebtedness exists, this will tend to lead to liquidation, through the alarm either of debtors or creditors or both. Then we may deduce the following chain of consequences in nine links:
>
> 1. Debt liquidation leads to distress selling and to
>
> 2. Contraction of deposit currency, as bank loans are paid off, and to a slowing down of velocity of circulation. This contraction of deposits and their velocity, precipitated by distress selling, causes
>
> 3. A fall in the level of prices, in other words a swelling of the dollar. Assuming, as above stated, that this fall of prices is not interfered with by reflation or otherwise, there must be
>
> 4. A still greater fall in the net worths of business, precipitating bankruptcies and
>
> 5. A like fall in profits, which in a 'capitalistic', that is, a private-profit society, leads the concerns which are running at a loss to make
>
> 6. A reduction in output, in trade and in employment of labor. These losses, bankruptcies, and unemployment, lead to
>
> 7. Pessimism and loss of confidence which in turn lead to
>
> 8. Hoarding [of money] and slowing down still more the velocity of circulation.
>
> The above eight changes cause
>
> 9. Complicated disturbances in the rates of interest, in particular, a fall in the nominal, or money, rates and a rise in the real, or commodity, rates of interest.

...Unless some counteracting cause comes along to prevent the fall in the price level, such a depression as that of 1929–33...tends to continue, going deeper, in a vicious spiral, for many years."
(Fisher, 1933)

It is quite remarkable how relevant Fisher's paper remains to the current macroeconomic situation. Fisher starts from "a state of over-indebtedness" and goes on to describe the economic depression caused by the ensuing self-reinforcing debt-deflation cycle. Fisher's analysis is an explicit contradiction of the neoclassical paradigm, in that it recognises the importance of a collective self-reinforcing effect as against the neoclassical individualist approach. The debt-deflation cycle is caused because individual decisions become synchronised and the resulting debt-deflation cycle pushes the economy away from the neoclassical equilibrium.

Had Fisher stopped his analysis at this point it would have been, for all practical purposes, indistinguishable from the Austrian school. However, where he heads next with his analysis opens up a substantive gulf between his paradigm and that of the Austrian school.

"...if the foregoing analysis is correct, *it is always economically possible to stop or prevent such a depression simply by reflating the price level* up to the average level at which outstanding debts were contracted by existing debtors and assumed by existing creditors, and then maintaining that level unchanged.

That the price level is controllable is not only claimed by monetary theorists but has recently been evidenced by two great events:

1. Sweden has now for nearly two years maintained a stable price level, practically always within 2 per cent of the chosen par and usually within 1 per cent...

2. The fact that immediate reversal of deflation is easily achieved by the use, or even the prospect use, of appropriate instrumentalities has just been demonstrated by President Roosevelt.

If reflation can now so easily and quickly reverse the deadly down-swing of deflation after nearly four years, when it was gathering increased momentum, it would have been still easier, and at any time, to have stopped it earlier.

I would emphasise the important corollary, of the debt-deflation theory, that *great depressions are curable and preventable through reflation and stabilisation.*" [Emphasis added]

Both Fisher and the Austrians agree on the destabilising effect of credit. Where they differ is in what to do about it. The Austrians say let the cycles run their course, while Fisher says prevent economic cycles with monetary policy. Fisher also asserts that this is an easily achievable goal – a big statement based on a little less than two years of Swedish inflation data!

Interestingly, it never appears to occur to Fisher that the wiser course of action may be to avoid accumulating the excess debt in the first place. By Fisher's logic there is no level of debt that is problematic because its detrimental effect can always be easily offset. It took about 50 years for Fisher's total disregard for debt to become the mainstream thinking in monetary policy circles. However, since the early 1980s the major central banks of the developed world have followed Fisher's policy prescription to the letter.

Recent events have been less than kind to Fisher's panglossian view of monetary policy: it has proven fiendishly difficult to reflate economies in the aftermath of major debt-deflation cycles. Nevertheless, Fisher's school of monetarism and the promotion of debt accumulation is now, and has been for a little over 30 years, the central element of macroeconomic policy in many developed economies.

7.1.4.2 Goodhart's law and the flaw in monetarism

Today's monetarist policies usually hide behind other names. This is largely because of the disastrous experiment with monetarism that occurred in Britain in the early 1980s. Under that particular flavour of monetarism, an effort was made to tightly control the amount of money in the economy in the belief that the money supply could be used to generate a steady rate of economic growth. For those interested in the details, I would recommend *The Rise and Fall of Monetarism* by the financial journalist David Smith (Smith, 1987). Smith captures the unscientific nature of monetarists quite eloquently:

> "Monetarists are a cunning lot. They will tell you that what they believe now is what they always believed and that the experience of the past several years has changed nothing. They will also tell you that events turned out in a way they had fully expected before the monetarist experiment got underway."

David Smith's account of the 1980s monetarist experiment is particularly enlightening because he describes both the events that led up to the experiment and how it went so quickly wrong. Smith notes that in the years prior to the experiment economists who studied monetary variables were able to make much more accurate predictions of economic activity than other economists. These monetarist economists believed the money supply controlled economic activity and therefore monitored it to measure and forecast economic activity. When they found that their forecasts were verified they naturally assumed that their thesis – money controls economic activity – was proven.

Policymakers also believed that their thesis was proven and decided to try controlling the economy with a rigid control of the money supply. However, when the experiment was actually tried, the economy did not perform as expected.

To understand what may have gone wrong, consider the following scenario:

A bright young economist begins studying the number of trucks travelling on the motorway system. After a short time a relationship becomes apparent between the number of trucks travelling in a given period and the subsequently reported level of economic activity. The economist concludes that road freight activity is a key driver of economic activity and promptly founds the freightist school of economics.

The freightist school lobbies the government to begin managing economic activity through the control of road freight. Policies are implemented to increase the number of trucks moving goods on the roads. Taxes affecting the haulage industry are cut and even schemes to subsidise the purchase and running of trucks are brought in.

The first results of the freightist experiment come in and they are positive; trucking levels increase and the economy grows – transportation costs have fallen, making companies more profitable. Naturally the government wants a bit more of this fine medicine and starts directly subsidising freight journeys. Eventually truckers start driving freight up and down the country just to harvest the subsidies. The economy stops growing but the freight statistics shoot through the roof. The relationship between economic activity and road freight breaks down.

What has happened is that the freightist school has mistaken the *direction* of the causality between road freight and economic activity. Stronger economic activity causes more road freight but more road freight does not necessarily cause more economic activity. For those of a philosophical bent, this confusion of cause and effect is one of Friedrich Nietzsche's four great philosophical errors that he says repeatedly cause mankind to misinterpret reality: "There is no more dangerous error than confounding consequence with cause: I call it the intrinsic depravity of reason." (Nietzsche, 1889)

Arguably, the monetarist school suffers from a bit of depravity of reason and commits the same analytical error as that of my fictitious freightist school. Money is a measure of credit, and credit, like truck journeys, is created and destroyed according to the prevailing economic activity. Money supply, in its various forms, is an excellent measure of economic activity when left alone. But it cannot be used as an instrument to control the economy and if it is used in this way it can no longer be used to measure the economy. This observation is what is known as Goodhart's law: "When a measure becomes a target, it ceases to be a measure."

Since the global financial crisis of 2008, central banks around the world have together deployed trillions of dollars of monetary stimulus in the form of policies known collectively as quantitative easing. These policies have had, at best, mixed results so far. It is sobering to contemplate that all of this money may have been spent based on a basic misunderstanding of cause and effect. To adapt Stalin: a billion wasted dollars is a tragedy; a trillion wasted dollars a statistic.

In writing this section I realised that the English language is missing a word. We need a new word to describe a situation in which it becomes necessary to extend a policy because to do otherwise would imply that the previous application of the policy had been in error and the consequences of acknowledging that error are too awful to contemplate. Such a word may already be applicable to quantitative easing and other tools designed to promote the accumulation of debt. I toyed with the idea of borrowing the recently minted term 'omnishambles', but this does not quite capture the self-perpetuating and self-reinforcing nature of the problem. Autoshambles may be more appropriate.

7.1.5 Keynesian school

John Maynard Keynes was a contemporary of Irving Fisher and like Fisher he offered a diagnosis of the Great Depression and a policy prescription for what to do about it. Keynes's analysis of the cause of the Great Depression was a little different to that of Fisher. Whereas Fisher emphasised the depressive, self-reinforcing dynamic caused by excess debt, Keynes focused on an equally self-reinforcing depressive dynamic which acted through spending.

Keynes described what he called a "paradox of thrift", whereby consumers collectively try to reduce their spending and increase their savings, only to find that the resultant depressive force on the economy causes their incomes to fall, thereby reducing their ability to save. This then induces further cuts in expenditure until the economy is driven into recession and eventually depression. This Keynesian analysis is, like the Austrian and monetarist analysis, an acknowledgement of collective destabilising forces at work in the economy and therefore another school of thought that rejects the neoclassical, individualist, equilibrium framework.

The Keynesian school, like Fisher's monetarist school, rejects the Austrian idea of allowing these destabilising forces to run their course. Where the Keynesians differ from the monetarists is in their recommended stabilisation policies. In essence, the monetarists argue that economic downturns should be countered by encouraging the private sector to increase activity through manipulating the level of private-sector debt higher with monetary tools – that is to say, by encouraging the private sector to borrow and spend. By contrast, the Keynesian school advocates replacing the 'missing' private sector activity with extra government spending – that is to say, by encouraging the government to borrow and spend.

On the face of it, there is little to choose between the Keynesian and monetarist paradigms: both argue for active macroeconomic management strategies and both, in practice, operate through borrowing money. The only difference is that the former aims to stimulate the economy by getting the government to borrow and spend, while the latter aims to do the same with the private sector. However, the philosophical difference between these strategies becomes stark when one contemplates what is implied for the size of the government sector by the Keynesian paradigm.

If the government is to vary its spending sufficiently to compensate for swings in private sector activity, it logically follows that government spending must be significant relative to the private sector. Therefore the Keynesian school implies substantial government spending and by necessity also substantial levels of taxation. For this reason, the Keynesian school is seen as a more profound challenge than monetarism to the combined positions of the neoclassical, libertarian and Austrian schools, which all believe in minimising the size of government.

7.1.6 Minsky's school

The American economist Hyman Minsky made an important observation that can be applied to both the Keynesian and monetarist arguments, and which also links back to both the neoclassical and Austrian schools.

Both Keynes and Fisher treated their respective destabilising 'paradox of thrift' and 'debt-deflation' cycles as events that occurred for reasons somehow outside of the economic system. Keynes did not explain why consumers might suddenly need to save and Fisher did not explain how the debt stock of an economy might become excessive. These were somehow external events, which just happened and then needed to be dealt with. This was helpful to the neoclassical paradigm, which could continue claiming that equilibrium was the normal state of affairs and everything that looked like disequilibrium could be treated as an external shock and therefore analysed as a special case.

In effect, Minsky took a closer look at the paradox of thrift and the debt-deflation cycle and realised that they both also worked in reverse. There was also a 'paradox of gluttony' and a 'debt-inflation' cycle. Minsky realised that in periods of stable economic activity, people will gain confidence and begin borrowing more money. This will result in them spending more money, which will create a stronger economy, leading to more confidence, more spending and more borrowing. Hey presto: the more that is consumed, the more that can be consumed – a paradox of gluttony!

Minsky's analysis amounts to a profound challenge to the neoclassical equilibrium idea, one that is much more troubling than either the Keynesian or monetarist paradigms. If Minsky's analysis is correct, and stability creates instability as he said, then it is impossible for the economy to remain in a stable equilibrium. Natural endogenous processes internal to the economy will tend to push the economy away from equilibrium into a cyclical boom-bust dynamic. In effect, Minsky had taken Keynsianism as a starting point and come back to a very Austrian analysis of the world.

Where Minsky and the Austrians differ is that Minsky thought that countercyclical policies could be used to stabilise these economic cycles. There is a degree of logical inconsistency in this position as, by Minsky's own analysis, these stabilising policies are likely to become self-defeating in the long run as they will eventually foster an unsustainable level of debt.

It is time to add Keynes's and Minsky's schools to the economic plane. I have placed the Keynesian school roughly at the centre of the economic plane, halfway up the Y-axis, reflecting its implicit suggestion that government activity needs to be comparable to private-sector activity and mid-way along the X-axis, reflecting its partial rejection of the idea of equilibrium. By contrast, I have placed the Minsky school at the far left of the X-axis, together with the Austrian school, reflecting its complete rejection of the equilibrium idea.

Figure 10: The economic plane with the addition of the Minsky and Keynesian schools of economics

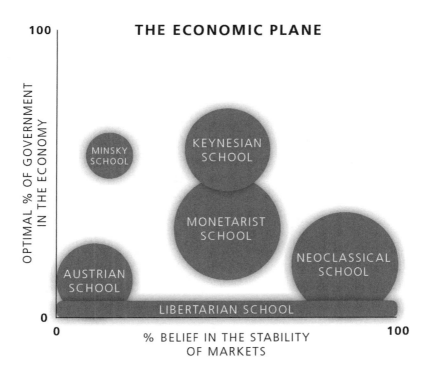

7.1.7 Marxist School

No survey of the schools of economic thought would be complete without covering Marxism which, despite its recent catastrophic collapse in the opinion polls, remains second only to Adam Smith's classical school in historical importance.

Marxism is yet another school of economic thought that argues that capitalism is an inherently unstable system. In this respect, Marxism is similar to the Austrian, Minsky, monetarist and the Keynesian schools of economics. Where Marxism differs from these schools is in what it identifies as the mechanism of capitalism's instability and its recommended remedy for the instability.

The Marxist instability mechanism is actually rather simple and for the most part in reasonable accordance with modern-day thinking. According to Marxism, profit is the result of being able to sell goods at a price higher than their cost of production. The gap between the cost of production and the sales price is what Marx called the "surplus value". In a competitive capitalist system, there would be fierce competition for the profits created by this surplus value. If one business was able to sell its goods reliably above the cost of production then a new business could, by adopting the same production techniques, enter the market and take the profits by undercutting the first business. As a result profits are only achieved by maintaining a "relative surplus value". In other words, businesses can only stay profitable, and capitalists can only stay rich, as long as they engage in a productivity arms race with their competitors.

From today's perspective, the fact that capitalists are forced to engage in a productivity arms race sounds like a very good idea indeed. Marx thought otherwise. According to Marx, this wicked competitive pressure would lead capitalists to seek productivity gains through innovation, which meant increased mechanisation. To Marx, who was never one to look on the bright side, this increased mechanisation meant fewer jobs and a greater share of the cost of production being diverted away from paying for workers (wages) toward the cost of paying for machinery (capital). As a result, workers would be forced into poverty and even capitalists would suffer. As the productivity arms race proceeded, the inevitable consequence would be to force smaller players out of business, leading to a monopolist position where profits and therefore wealth became concentrated into the hands of an ever smaller elite.

In Marx's own words:

> "Along with the constantly diminishing number of the magnates of capital, who usurp and monopolise all advantages of this process of transformation, grows the mass of misery, oppression, slavery, degradation, exploitation; but with this too grows the revolt of the working class, a class always increasing in numbers." (Marx, 1867)

The key points of capitalism leading to an impoverished working class, a concentration of wealth in the hands of monopolists and revolution, were not lost on Lenin who offered his own summary of Marxism along the following lines:

> "Capital, created by the labour of the worker, crushes the worker, ruining small proprietors and creating an army of unemployed... By destroying small-scale production, capital leads to an increase in productivity of labour and to the creation of a monopoly position for the associations of big capitalists...Capitalism has triumphed all over the world, but this triumph is only the prelude to the triumph of labour over capital." (Lenin, 1913)

Of course, Marx thought that this process of wealth polarisation would inevitably lead to the downtrodden working class rising up in revolt to replace capitalism with an egalitarian society in which everyone would work harmoniously together and share the output equally. Marx believed this new system would take "from each according to his ability" and give "to each according to his needs".

It is fascinating to see both Marx and Lenin acknowledging that capitalism leads to rising productivity but choosing to interpret this as a bad thing. Viewed from today's perspective, it is easy to see where Marx's analysis went so badly wrong. He was suffering from what we call today the 'lump of labour fallacy'. This is the idea that there is a fixed amount of work to be done in the economy so that any new entrants to the labour market, be they man or machine, will lead to a rise in unemployment.

What the lump of labour argument misses, of course, is that extra workers also means extra customers. The economy is not a fixed system but a highly adaptive one. Marx failed to see that workers would be needed to manufacture the machines that were required for this productivity arms race. What's more, these new workers would need to be better skilled, better educated and better paid than those they replaced. Marx also missed the rather obvious fact that the capitalists, who were in a productivity arms race, would be producing more things and would therefore need more customers and those customers must, eventually, be their own workers.

We can now say with some confidence that Marx was wholly wrong in his belief that competition, innovation and rising productivity causes poverty and unemployment. Viewed at the economy-wide level, the process causes *redeployment* rather than unemployment. What's more, the redeployment is toward higher-skilled, better-paid jobs. This is not to say that some lower-skilled workers may lose out in the transition process, but at the level of the aggregate economy, which is what Marx claimed to be studying, the effect is very much higher rather than lower living standards. In essence, the Marxist analysis of productivity and industrialisation was even less sophisticated than that of the Luddite or Saboteur movements, who at least appreciated that they were simply trying to hold onto their existing menial jobs.[15]

The Marxist school's critique of the implications of productivity gains can be dismissed as badly misguided. On the other hand, Marx's argument that capitalism has an inherent tendency toward wealth

---

[15] In 19th century England the Luddites were a group of weavers who attempted to protect their jobs and resist the trend toward mechanisation by destroying mechanised weaving looms. The term saboteur is believed to arise from a similar Dutch/French movement, where the chosen method of sabotaging the machinery was to throw their wooden clogs, *sabots*, into the workings of the loom. Hence the term sabotage.

polarisation cannot be dismissed so easily. There are very good reasons for believing that the Marxist school may be correct in claiming that capitalism has an inbuilt tendency toward both monopoly power and wealth polarisation.

The tendency of capitalism to seek to mitigate the profit-depleting effect of competition through establishing monopolistic or oligopolistic arrangements is something both Karl Marx and Adam Smith recognised. To quote Smith on the topic: "People of the same trade seldom meet together, even for merriment and diversion, but the conversation ends in a conspiracy against the public, or in some contrivance to raise prices." (Smith A., 1776)

The problem of anticompetitive monopolistic practice as identified by both Smith and Marx has long been recognised in all major developed economies: America has its anti-trust legislation, the UK its Competition Commission and the European Union its Antitrust and Mergers Commissions. None of these institutions would be necessary were it not for the reality that capitalism does suffer an inherent tendency toward monopoly and wealth polarisation.

The issue of wealth polarisation has recently re-emerged as a hot topic for both academic economists and policymakers. Recent studies have shown that over the last three decades the developed economies of the US, UK and Europe have experienced a marked polarisation of income and wealth. Studies, especially of the US economy, show that since the start of the 1980s the income of the wealthiest section of society has risen sharply both in absolute terms and also as a share of overall income. In a recent paper, 'Striking it Richer', Emmanuel Saez of UC Berkeley noted that:

> "From 2009 to 2012, average real income per family grew modestly by 6%...However, the gains were very uneven. The top 1% of incomes grew by 31.4% while the bottom 99% of incomes grew only by 0.4% from 2009 to 2012." (Saez, 2013)

Saez's data shows some fascinating developments in the distribution of incomes for US households over the last 100 years. Interestingly, in the 1920s and 30s the top 10% of US households used to take home around 45% of all income. This fell to around 33% after the second world war, where it remained until the start of the 1980s. However, since the start of the 1980s, the growth of the incomes of the top 10% has been continually outstripping the rest of society, and now they take home a little over 50% of all income.

This trend of wealth polarisation is controversial on a number of levels. In academic circles there is much argument about why it has happened and in policy circles over what, if anything, should be done about it and what it means for the economy.

The issue of the distribution of wealth is, I would argue, another area that marks economics out as being in a state of scientific crisis: mainstream economics says remarkably little on the topic and many economists appear to believe it is a subject outside the realm of economics. By contrast, most outside of the profession would expect such an issue to be central to the field. In a sense the issue of wealth distribution is to economics what the jigsaw puzzle of the continents was to geology – a problem that is so obviously central to the field but nonetheless left unexplained and undiscussed.

We must now place Marxism on the economic plane. As Marx thought capitalism must inevitably collapse, he obviously rejected the neoclassical idea that capitalism is a naturally stable system. Therefore Marxism must go on the far left of the plane. Similarly, as Marx thought the only way to address capitalism's problems was to abandon it altogether and replace the whole capitalist system with a socialist system, Marxism must be placed at the very top of the Y-axis, representing 100% government control of the economy. This puts Marxism in the top left of the plane, as far away from the neoclassical school – in the bottom right – as it is possible to be. In this sense, Marxism is the antithesis of the neoclassical thesis.

Figure 11: The economic plane with the addition of the Marxist school of economics

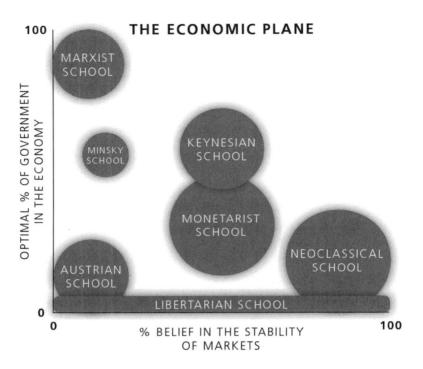

We have two more important schools of economic thought to cover – the behavioural and institutional schools. Unfortunately, neither of these fit onto the economic plane at all.

7.2 Behavioural School

The Austrian, monetarist, Keynesian and Minsky schools of economics all challenge the neoclassical school in similar ways. In each case there is a mechanism that causes collective behaviour rather than individualistic behaviour, in contravention of the first axiom of the neoclassical school. This collective behaviour then leads to decision-making that, though rational on an individual basis, turns out to be irrational at the aggregate level, violating the second axiom of the neoclassical school, which requires only optimal welfare-maximising decisions. Finally, this non-maximising herding behaviour then violates the third axiom of the neoclassical school by driving the economy away from equilibrium.

The behavioural school of economics challenges the core axioms of the neoclassical school in a different, more direct, way. This school has shown through experimental evidence that individuals do not always make what economists judge to be rational welfare-maximising decisions. Furthermore, they do not always act independently. There is one particularly famous experiment from the behavioural school that causes special anxiety for supporters of the neoclassical school and which I wish to develop in the next chapter. This experiment is known as the ultimatum game and it works as follows.

Two players are told they will share a sum of money between them, provided they can agree on how it is to be split. If they cannot agree the split then both players receive nothing. One of the players is allowed to make just a single offer to the other player as to how to divide up the money. The other player must then accept or reject that offer. Once that offer is accepted or rejected, the money is either paid or retained and the game is over.

According to the neoclassical paradigm, where everyone acts independently to maximise their own welfare, what should happen is that the first player offers only a small share of the money to the second player. The second player, who then has a simple choice between the small payment or no payment at all, will then accept the small offer and the first player will get to keep the bulk of the money.

In practice, what usually happens is quite different. If the first player makes a very low offer then the second player frequently rejects the offer, choosing to get nothing at all. The second player appears to act irrationally in choosing to punish himself or herself in order to inflict a greater punishment on the first player. More frequently, perhaps because this punishment is anticipated, the first player makes an offer closer to an even split of the money, and this near-even split is accepted.

The ultimatum game is verifiable empirical evidence of behaviour that contradicts the neoclassical paradigm. According to Francis Bacon's theory of the scientific method, this should cause the neoclassical paradigm to be immediately rejected. In practice, of course, this has not happened and instead economists have done what Thomas Kuhn suggested they would do: they have put it down as an interesting oddity and continued on as before. They have done this for the simple reason that, without an alternative paradigm to explain this behaviour, they have no other choice.

So far economics is treating the growing body of evidence against humans behaving as rational optimisers as problematic, inexplicable and annoying – but also ignorable. This is the same pattern of behaviour exhibited by geologists prior to Wegener's theory – recall that at that time geologists believed the earth was solid rock, leading them to largely ignore the very obvious implications of seismic and volcanic activity.

What was necessary to get geologists to start contemplating that the earth's core might really be molten was a story that made that possibility comprehensible – the discovery of heat generated by radioactive decay was the necessary story. What is now needed to get mainstream economics to integrate the ideas of the behavioural school into its theories is a story that makes the results of experiments like the ultimatum game also comprehensible. In the next chapter I will suggest a small shift in perspective that makes the behaviour of players in the ultimatum game look much more rational.

7.3 Institutional School

The final school of economic philosophy that I wish to mention is the now largely ignored institutional school. To understand where the institutional school is coming from, consider the following thought experiment.

Imagine yourself as an astronaut looking down on the earth from your spaceship. You are looking at the dark side of the earth and watching as it slowly turns beneath you. For the most part the surface is in total darkness, except for the occasional pockets of light marking out the larger cities and conurbations. Large parts of Europe and the Mediterranean rim are illuminated, Japan and much of the Pacific Rim can be picked out, as can the east and west coasts of North America and a few specks in Africa and South America.

Now imagine that you were able to watch this same picture like a fast-forwarded movie. For argument's sake, let us imagine the whole of the last 10,000 years of history, from the end of the Stone Age through to the present day, could be condensed into a movie of the earth from space, lasting just 60 minutes.

Aside from the occasional volcanic eruption or flash of lightning, the first 59 ½ minutes of the movie would be entirely black. Then at about 30 seconds before the credits roll, there would be the faintest flickering of light as the earliest electric street lights go on.[16] Over the course of the next 30 seconds these tiny pinpricks of light would spread like wildfire around the globe until, in the final second of the movie, essentially all of the major conurbations of the earth are illuminated at night by electricity. Why did the lights suddenly go on in the last 30 seconds of the movie? Why did they start in Europe and North America?

Admittedly this thought experiment is somewhat biased by its focus on the single technology of the electric street light. So imagine instead that, somehow the same 60-minute movie could be made showing just periods of economic growth. Let's say, for argument's sake, that anywhere on earth that was experiencing a significant improvement in human living standards from one generation to the next could be made to light up. Now you would see the occasional flashes of light throughout the last 15 minutes of the movie. But they would be very short indeed. Even the long-lived Egyptian, Roman and Chinese civilisations had only the briefest periods in which living standards improved, followed by centuries

---

[16] The first electric street lights were in the North East of England, a very fine area of the world. To be precise they were on Mosely Street, Newcastle upon Tyne, and were turned on in 1879.

of stagnation and decline. Only in the last minute would there be anywhere where the light of progress went on and stayed on for any protracted period. And only in the last 30 seconds would the light start to spread to large areas of the world.

This thought experiment helps illustrate just how abnormal the last few centuries of economic progress have been.

You would think that economics would have rather a lot to say about this occurrence. It does not. In practice, the whole growth story is a huge problem for the mainstream schools of economics. Recall that the neoclassical, libertarian and Austrian schools all advocate a philosophy in which economic growth arises through individual pursuit of self-interest, with government regulations and taxation considered as an impediment to what would otherwise be a better, more natural, state of affairs. These are fine arguments. Until, that is, you pause to remember that small government, light regulation and low taxation is the economic condition that has persisted across most of the world through all of history. Why then has the world not been plagued by a permanent growth-boom lasting thousands of years?

If economic progress is really down to just competition and the pursuit of self-interest, forces which as Stigler put it are Newtonian in their universality, then mainstream economics has a problem. Indeed, if we follow the logic of the neoclassical, libertarian or Austrian schools, all of which see big government as an impediment to economic progress, then the last 100 years of history should have been an especially growth-free zone for America and Europe.

Something does not quite stack up when you look at economic theory and economic history. Are we to believe that 14th century Europeans did not pursue self-interest, while 19th century Europeans did? Are we to believe that the street vendors of Mumbai, Nairobi and Rio de Janeiro pursue their own self-interest with any less vigour than do the investment bankers of London, New York or Hong Kong? Why did medieval Europeans make such little progress while Victorian era Europeans moved forward in leaps and bounds? Why do slum-dwelling street vendors fight so vigorously for every sale and yet make no economic progress?

The problem for mainstream economic theory is that the experimental evidence suggests that the way we choose to arrange our societies has enormous influence on how our economies actually work. However, there is simply no coherent way to integrate this observation into the neoclassical paradigm, which attempts to construct its theories based on an assumed universal model of humans as individualist, welfare-maximising machines. In the neoclassical paradigm, for example, there is no way to ask: Are we modelling a communist consumer or a capitalist consumer? In the neoclassical paradigm this is a nonsense question, like a physicist asking: Am I modelling a communist atom or a capitalist atom?

I am fairly certain that there is no behavioural difference between communist and capitalist atoms, but I'm not so sure the same can be said of consumers – not least because there is usually precious little for communist consumers to consume. This is a stark example of Kuhn's incommensurability problem. The institutional economists want to discuss questions that cannot be addressed in the neoclassical paradigm.

Economic growth is another example of the jigsaw puzzle problem in economics, another huge topic that is clearly central to the field but which goes unexplained and undiscussed. This is where the institutional school of economics steps in.

The institutional school of economics does not believe economies can be understood simply with laws derived from assumptions about human behaviour. Instead they believe that it is also necessary to understand the structures, institutions, laws and norms of the economy and society more broadly. To the institutional school, the question of why the growth light was suddenly turned on means asking what changed in the institutional framework of the economy to make that possible?

The problem for mainstream economics is that when we start asking why economies grow, the thinking starts to go something like this:

Q: What do the richest economies in the world have in common?
A: Strong democracies, good rule of law and large governments.

Q: What do the poorest countries have in common?
A: Weak or missing democracies, poor rule of law and small governments – or sometimes very large governments.

Q: What happened at around the time economies began to grow?
A: Societies started becoming more democratic, the rule of law improved and governments got larger.

Conclusion: Democracy, law and government are part of the process of getting rich.

This leads to a clash of ideology between, especially, the neoclassical, libertarian and Austrian schools and the institutional school. To paraphrase President Reagan – for neoclassical economists, government is always part of the problem; whereas for institutional economists, government looks suspiciously like part of the solution.

A small cohort of the mainstream neoclassical school has attempted to tackle the embarrassing problem of growth with an ingeniously disingenuous piece of logic. It goes as follows: If a country happens to be rich and it also happens to be a democracy then the people will vote for large governments. Therefore rich democracies have large governments. But the large governments play no part in making them rich.

This line of reasoning leads to what is known as the growth-first democracy-later model in which, remarkably, democracy is portrayed as an impediment to growth and a luxury that can only be afforded once a country has already become rich. This argument is discussed in *The Democracy Advantage* by Morton Halperin et al. (Halperin et al., 2004). An obvious counterpoint that challenges this line of reasoning is, of course, the fact that today's rich economies did not first become rich and then democratise; rather, they democratised first (albeit initially only partially) and then became rich. The journey towards prosperity went hand in hand with the journey towards democracy.

A simple common-sense look at history and the most successful of today's economies says that democracy has to be part of the story of economic progress. The problem of integrating democracy and its associated larger governments into the narrative of the neoclassical and other schools has unfortunately led to democracy being neglected and almost completely airbrushed out of the narrative of economic success. Given the empirical evidence, it is unscientific not to at least consider whether democracy and government play a role in the promotion of economic growth. The failure to address this point is another symptom of economics being in a scientific crisis.

7.4 The Problem of Herding Economists

The very fact that there are so many disparate schools of economics both on and off our economic plane is a symptom that all is not well in the field of economics. A further aspect of the problem is inconsistency over time. Up to this point I have described the neoclassical school as the consensus opinion. This is true today, but it was not always the case. We could imagine the economic plane as a real plane populated with all of the economists in the world. Over the last century or so there would have been some considerable migrations around the plane – I have in my mind's eye something that looks like the herds of wildebeest on the East African Serengeti.

In the 1930s through to the 60s, the bulk of the herd would have been clustered around the Keynesian school, with substantial populations in the Marxist, Austrian and neoclassical quarters. In the 1970s, there would have been a migration away from the Marxist and towards the monetarist areas. From the 1980s onwards, the drift would have been increasingly toward the entire herd moving into the neoclassical quadrant.

In 2008, as Lehman Brothers was failing, there would have been a stampede away from the neoclassical quarter towards the Minsky zone as everyone suddenly rejected the silly notion of an inherently stable economy and embraced Minsky's idea of an inherently unstable economy.

At around this time the term "Minsky moment"[17] became briefly fashionable. In the years since 2008, Minsky has been forgotten and the herd has quickly drifted back to recolonise the neoclassical zone, conveniently forgetting that it ever left.

This continual migration between different schools of thought is another indication that economics is acting unscientifically and that none of the schools of thought are sufficiently convincing to maintain their dominance for long.

It also provides another powerful defensive mechanism for the profession as a whole. Because economic ideas move in and out of fashion so freely over time, anyone wishing to critique the views of a given school finds themselves engaged in a futile game of whack-a-mole.

7.5 Computational Complexity

The final piece of evidence I shall cite to support the argument of economics being in crisis is to draw a comparison between the state of mathematical modelling in economics today and the Ptolemaic models of the universe before Copernicus. Consider the passages from a recent paper from the chief economist of the International Monetary Fund, Olivier Blanchard, in which he extolls the progress of economic models:

> "The most visible outcomes of this new approach are the dynamic stochastic general *equilibrium models* (or DSGEs). They are models derived from micro foundations – that is utility maximisation by consumers-workers, value maximisation by firms, rational expectations, and a full specification of imperfections, from nominal rigidities to some of the imperfections discussed earlier and typically estimated by Bayesian methods. The result of estimation is a set of structural parameters fully characterising the

---

[17] The Minsky moment is the point at which a self-reinforcing credit expansion turns into a self-reinforcing credit contraction. Or alternatively when the paradox of gluttony turns into a paradox of thrift, or the debt-inflation cycle becomes the debt-deflation cycle.

model. *The number of parameters has been steadily increasing with the power of computers*: Smets and Wouters (2007) for example estimate 19 structural parameters and 17 parameters corresponding to the variances and the first order autocorrelation coefficients of the underlying shock processes...DSGE models have become ubiquitous. Dozens of teams of researchers are involved in their construction. Nearly every central bank has one, or wants to have one." (Blanchard, 2008)

Note the pride taken not just in the rising number of parameters in the models but also in the growing number of versions of the models. If economics is really a universal science, should we have different models for different places? If the laws of economics are Newtonian in their universality, then one universal model should do. Would we have considered Einstein's general theory of relativity a triumph if he had replaced Newtonian gravity with a model with 19 structural parameters and 17 variances and which only described gravity, incorrectly, in Switzerland?

Dynamic stochastic general equilibrium models may be on the verge of describing our economies accurately. Maybe with just a few dozen more free variables, a handful of epicycles, and a super computer the size of Deep Thought we will be able to model the economy. Alternatively, the growing complexity of these models and their proliferation in number, without any obvious improvements in their explanatory power, may be a mirror of what happened during the dark ages of Ptolemaic astronomy. We may need simpler theories, fewer variables and a Copernican-style shift in perspective instead.

7.6 Conclusion

Hopefully, with this chapter, I have convinced you that not everything is quite as it should be in the 'science' of economics. If I have achieved this much, I will consider this book a success – if for no other reason than the pronouncements emanating from any field riven with this degree of internal conflict and inconsistency should be treated with a great deal of scepticism.

That said, as mentioned earlier, Thomas Kuhn's analysis of how science works in practice threw up the unexpected finding that we do not reject a theory just because we know it to be wrong. Kuhn's work suggested that we will, if not happily then at least reluctantly, continue using even a thoroughly refuted theory until a better one comes along. For this reason, throwing stones at the various schools of economics as I have done here is of little practical value unless it is also possible to offer a better paradigm to displace the old one.

The next chapters focus on the search for a better way to look at our economic system, a new perspective that helps clear up some of the problems discussed in this chapter. Kuhn gave us some useful hints as to what a good paradigm shift should do. He said it was not about finding new data: it was about reinterpreting what we already know from a fresh perspective. It is about preserving the best, seemingly incompatible, ideas of the previous schools of thought and rearranging them in a new way that makes them more coherent. Above all, Kuhn said it was about *conceptual efficiency* – telling a simple story about how the world works, which helps us think more efficiently and see things more clearly.

In looking for the necessary paradigm shift, I am going to ruthlessly plagiarise the masters. The first step is to borrow Charles Darwin's big idea and use that to explain how the natural human economy really works, and why economic growth is very much not the normal state of affairs. The second step is to borrow both William Harvey's big idea and his conceptual trick and use these to explain what we have done to the natural Darwinian system to make economic growth the new normal state of affairs.

The upshot of marrying the ideas of Darwin and Harvey is a very simple paradigm shift toward a model of the economy that looks suspiciously like that of Alfred Wegener's big idea.

8 BORROWING FROM MR DARWIN

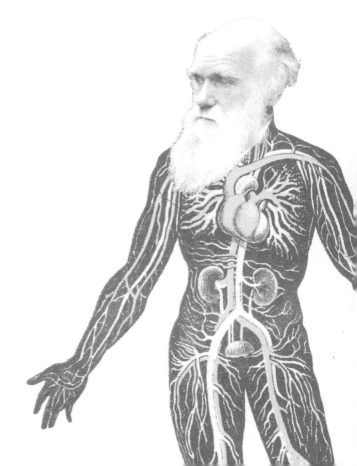

"It may be taken as the consensus…that economics is helplessly behind the times, and unable to handle its subject matter in a way to entitle it to standing as a modern science."

Thorstein Veblen (Veblen, 1898)

IN THE MIDDLE of the 19th century, Charles Darwin borrowed a couple of ideas from two economists to help him unravel the problem of evolution. He took the idea of productivity improvements, arising through specialisation, from Adam Smith, and he got the idea of competition between individuals within a species from the insights of Thomas Malthus. Malthus had explained the bleak implications of our reproductive arithmetic and in so doing planted the seed of the idea of natural selection through competition. In this chapter we are going to turn things full circle and use Darwin's big idea to look at economics afresh.

8.1 The Ultimate Competitor

Anyone who has watched Usain Bolt, the men's 100-metre Olympic champion, race cannot help but admire his style. Typically he starts the race a little slower than the rest of the field. By about the halfway mark he is surging past his rivals, and by the time he is in the last ten metres of the race he is often turning around to check just how far the rest of the field are behind him. Often he then appears to ease up and almost saunter across the line in first place. It is a beautiful thing to behold.

Why does Bolt race in this way? Why does he check his position in the field? Why does he appear to ease up once he is confident of victory? Why do we admire him for it?

No one could deny that Usain Bolt is anything other than a supreme example of the competitive human machine. On the face of it, his behaviour should be a near-perfect fit for the competitive models so beloved of the neoclassical school of economics. But Bolt does not behave according to the neoclassical model. Were he to do so he would run as fast as he could right up to the line. As a neoclassical competitor, Bolt would never ease up once he was comfortably in the lead. A perfect neoclassical competitor would always seek to maximise his performance, in Bolt's case by minimising his time in each race.

To be fair, we could torture the neoclassical maximisation paradigm a bit and make it fit Bolt's behaviour. We could say, for example: Bolt wishes to maximise the number of races he wins over his athletic career and therefore does not risk straining his body further once he is assured of victory. Alternatively, we could recognise that there is a subtle difference between maximisation behaviour and competitive behaviour. Maximising or optimising behaviour, as economists like to term it, involves seeking to attain the best possible outcome in absolute terms. I'm sure Bolt does just this in the races in which he is seeking to set a world record. On the other hand competitive behaviour is fundamentally a relative game. Bolt as a competitor is seeking to run faster than the other runners, regardless of his absolute speed.

The neoclassical economists often talk of their models as representing competitive processes and often argue that their theories are built in accordance with the natural competitive forces recognised by Charles Darwin. But when they come to actually do the mathematics, they do not model competition; they model maximisation. There is a very good reason for modelling the economy using the assumption of maximisation rather than competition. Modelling maximising behaviour is trivial, modelling competitive behaviour is fiendishly difficult.

Let's say, for example, that you want to build a model to predict Usain Bolt's next 100m time. If you wished to model this as a neoclassical economist would, you might take the results of his last ten races, plot the results on a chart and take the average. If you wanted to be a bit more sophisticated, you might even fit a line through the points and extrapolate his next result. Either way, all you need to know about is Bolt himself. On the other hand, if you want to model Bolt as a competitor you need to know about everyone he is racing against. If he is racing against the second-, third- and fourth-fastest sprinters in the world, your model should predict a time that is just a bit faster than any of those runners could run. If he's running against three blokes he happened to meet last night in the pub, the model should predict a much slower time. But then again, if one of the people in the pub happened to be fellow Jamaican sprinter Yohan Blake, the model would have to be adjusted again.

Hopefully the point is clear. Modelling a system in which each of the components are engaged in maximising behaviour is relatively simple, modelling a system in which each of the components is engaged in competitive behaviour is very difficult, and at the level of the economy effectively impossible. In a competitive system, the actions of each individual component are dependent on those of all the others. Not only is more data required, but spontaneous complicated group behaviour, feedback effects and herding all become real possibilities.

The core idea of the neoclassical school of economics is to build mathematical models to describe the economy based on fundamental principles. It is worth revisiting those principles:

1. Individualism: people make their decisions independently of one another based on their own self-interest.

2. Maximisation: the decisions made by individuals are always designed to maximise their own welfare.

3. Equilibrium: the result of all of these individual optimising decisions is a stable system in optimal equilibrium.

Consider for a moment what happens if we replace maximisation with competition. Competition, as discussed, is fundamentally a relative not an individualistic process. So the first principle of individual decision making will have to be discarded. But if we introduce competition and discard individualism can we be sure of retaining equilibrium?

So we have a problem with the neoclassical school of economics that is quite fundamental. The problem lies not with the details of its models but with its core axioms. If we humans really behave as competitors rather than optimisers, all three of the axioms of mainstream economics are simply wrong. Recall that when Copernicus changed only one of the two axioms of Ptolemaic astronomy he ended up changing the whole of the science of astronomy. If we adopt a Darwinian competitive paradigm we have to change all three of the axioms of economics at once.[18]

8.2 Are We Competitors Or Optimisers?

It is not going to be easy to prove that it is better to model human decision-making with a competitive rather than an optimising model. That said, the burden of proof should lie with the neoclassical school to demonstrate that we humans exhibit *no* element of Darwinian competitive behaviour, because that is what is required to retain the axioms of neoclassical economics. What we can do is to consider some of the evidence in favour of viewing humans as Darwinian competitors, do a few thought experiments and then ask ourselves which is the more reasonable assumption: considering ourselves as Darwinian competitors or as neoclassical optimisers.

8.2.1 Darwin

If we accept, as I suspect most of us do, that humans are the product of a long succession of evolutionary pressures, then we must logically concede that we have inherited traits from our ancestors. Furthermore, we must accept that our ancestors had to compete with their peers for resources in order to survive and that we are the product of whichever humans happened to be the best competitors. Darwinian evolution is therefore itself the most powerful reason to believe that we have evolved an innately competitive spirit. Certainly we are smart enough to coordinate our decisions into cooperative rather than competitive behaviour, but even this is often to foster competition at a group level rather than an individual level.

---

[18] This is why, in chapter 7, I did not dwell on the issue of whether the third 'equilibrium axiom' is really an independent axiom in its own right or a result of the other two axioms. If we are Darwinian competitors, it does not matter: all three axioms must be discarded.

When we were evolving on the planes of Africa into the tribal, social animals that we are, was it more important that we were able to run fast or that we could run faster than our neighbour? My guess is that when a lion was looking for lunch, the most important thing was not to run fast; it was to run faster than the person next to you. That is to say, it was the ability to *compete successfully* that ensured survival.

8.2.2 The ultimatum game

In the previous chapter I mentioned the apparently puzzling results of the ultimatum game. As a reminder, in the ultimatum game an amount of money is divided between two players provided they can agree on the split. If they cannot agree, they both get nothing. The first player is able to make only one proposal of how to divide the money and the other player must either accept the proposal or reject it. Rejection results in neither getting anything.

Neoclassical economists, working to an optimising paradigm, have puzzled over why the second player tends to reject small offers and why the first player typically makes offers that appear overly generous. Viewed from a competitive rather than an optimising paradigm, this behaviour looks much less odd.

The second player will reject an offer in which the split of the money is especially uneven, because this result will give the first player a substantial competitive advantage. The first player instinctively understands this psychology and therefore offers to split the money more evenly. The first player's motivation is to make an offer that retains only as much relative advantage as the second player will tolerate. In effect, the first player is trying to find the point at which the second player's desire for wealth maximisation just barely exceeds their intolerance of relative disadvantage.

8.2.3 The hedonic treadmill

Another interesting experimental observation of human behaviour, which comes out of both psychology and experimental economics, is known as the hedonic treadmill. The hedonic treadmill is a term used to describe the apparent mean-reverting behaviour of happiness.

In other words, it has been observed that when people experience either large positive or negative shocks – the kind that would be expected to materially change their level of happiness – the effect is often only temporary. For example, people who win the lottery apparently feel temporarily elated, but after some time has gone by their level of happiness returns to roughly where it was before the win. Similarly, people who suffer permanent traumatic injury often feel temporarily depressed but over time recover from this.

One simple way to understand this phenomenon is to recognise that we are instinctively competitive. We measure ourselves and derive our happiness from our relative position to our peers. The lottery winners feel immediate happiness as they become richer than their peers. But as they move out of their old neighbourhood into better areas they acquire new, wealthier, peers and as a result their relative competitive position falls back and so therefore does their happiness.

The hedonic treadmill is therefore an excellent description of human nature. We strive to better our condition, believing that we will become happier as a result. But once we become better off we find we are still next to people doing just as well as us; we shift our perspective and our happiness then falls back as we start to look at those just ahead of us again. Because we are innately competitive, we are on a hedonic treadmill running to get ahead but at the same time staying still.

8.2.4 The fashion and luxury industries and Veblen goods

One of the core theories of economics that emerges as a consequence of our assumed desire to maximise wealth is the inverse relationship between the price of a good and the demand for that good. According to the law of supply and demand, as the price of a good rises people start looking around for alternatives – thereby causing demand for that good to fall back. This is the key mechanism by which neoclassical economists believe market-based systems maintain equilibrium. However, the economist Thorstein Veblen noted that the demand for some goods, particularly luxuries, does not obey the law of supply and demand. For some luxuries, demand actually rises with price – fine wine, jewellery, designer clothes all spring to mind.

The price-demand behaviour of these Veblen goods cannot be explained by the wealth-maximising paradigm of the neoclassical school. But they *can* be explained by a competitive paradigm, whereby the purpose of the good is to signal a relative position in society. The purchase of expensive positional goods makes little sense without recognising our inherently competitive nature.

For this reason it may be argued that the entire fashion and luxury industries, in all of their superficially irrational glory, are hard empirical evidence that we are primarily competitors rather than optimisers.

8.3 Some Thought Experiments on Competition vs Optimisation

The following are two thought experiments that may help you decide, for yourself, if you are an optimiser or a competitor:

The pay rise

Imagine you work as part of a team of ten people. The team is itself part of a much bigger company, with, say, 1,000 employees.

One day your boss announces to the team that the company is so happy with the team's work that the team is to get an average pay rise of 20%, while the rest of the company's employees will get only a 10% raise.

How do you feel in response to this news? Most likely you feel quite happy.

Next your boss calls you into the office and tells you your individual pay rise. You are told that you will be getting a 15% increase.

You now know that you're doing better than the rest of the organisation but also that you're doing worse than your immediate peers. How do you feel in response to this news? Be honest!

Anyone who has ever been involved in setting compensation levels for teams will be very aware that the angst is almost always about *relative* rather than absolute issues. This is why human resource departments go to such lengths to keep pay-levels confidential.

The new car

You live in a street of identical houses. You and your neighbours drive identical cars. You trade in your ten-year-old Ford for a shiny new BMW 5 Series. When you get home that night you leave your new car outside the garage for your neighbours to see. How do you feel as you go to bed that night?

You wake up the next morning, go out to the car and see that your neighbours have all got shiny new BMW 7 Series, all of which are considerably more expensive than your new car. Do you feel delighted for them? Be honest!

8.4 Darwin Refutes Marx and Smith

I am now going to argue that if we accept that human behaviour is inherently competitive then we must reject all of the classical, neoclassical, libertarian, Austrian and Marxist schools of economics. The reasons for rejecting the classical, neoclassical and Marxist schools of economics are, I think, quite obvious, so I shall cover those first. The reasons for rejecting the Austrian and libertarian schools are much more interesting and more helpful in suggesting a way forward for economics.

8.4.1 Darwin vs the neoclassical school of economics

The problems caused by Darwinian competition for the neoclassical school of economics have already been covered above, so I shall recapitulate only very briefly.

If human decision-making is fundamentally a competitive process, then decisions of individuals become dependent upon those of their peers. This implies that behaviour at the aggregate level of the economy cannot be reliably modelled as the sum of individual behaviours. Nor can it be safely assumed that the behaviour of individuals in competition will lead to an equilibrium situation. Indeed it is likely that competitive actors will always seek to disturb any equilibrium. The naïve, neoclassical approach of modelling macroeconomic systems as the sum of the behaviour of independent individuals therefore fails.

8.4.2 Darwin vs Marxism

Arguably, Darwinian competition is in accordance with Marx's bleak view of capitalism as an unstable wealth-polarising system (more on this in a moment). However, Darwinism is in stark contradiction to the system that Marx thought should replace capitalism. If we are indeed motivated by our position relative to our peers, then any economic system (such as communism) which attempts to reallocate resources evenly, without regard to an individual's contribution to the system, would be wholly abhorrent to human nature.

Many economists have criticised Marxism because it does not use the pricing mechanism to allocate resources. They argue that the free-market system naturally achieves the optimal allocation of resources and thereby maximises the welfare of society as a whole. Since this free-market allocation of resources is assumed to be perfect, any other, non-free market system must be inferior. If, as I have argued above, this neoclassical optimisation construct is flawed and has to be replaced with a competitive paradigm, then it is no longer safe to assume that a free-market system automatically achieves the best possible utilisation of resources.

One could, for example, imagine a situation in which, due to herding behaviour, resource-utilisation became skewed in suboptimal ways for extended periods. For example – gold may become an excessively fashionable investment, leading to a socially unproductive deployment of resources tasked with relocating gold from underground mines in Africa to underground vaults in Switzerland.

As a thought experiment, let us imagine that with today's powerful computers it was possible to design a centrally planned economic system that could achieve an output level twice as high as an imperfect, unstable free-market system. And now let's imagine that the wealth of this centrally planned system is divided equally amongst the workers along communist lines. What would the likely response be to this fixed reward system, if we really are naturally competitive?

As we could not compete on the output of the system – that is, the rewards – we would naturally start to compete on the inputs, the work. The only way to gain a competitive upper hand relative to our peers would be to receive the same fixed benefit for a *lower* amount of work. In this way we would at least enjoy a greater benefit per unit of work. Of course, the result would be a race to the bottom, with everyone competing to do less than each other – we call this demotivation. Eventually the system would collapse under the weight of demotivation until management, or the politburo, resorted to coercion. Unfortunately for many millions of people in the communist bloc, over many years, this was a very real situation, not just a thought experiment.

If we are really Darwinian competitors, we must accept an uneven distribution of rewards as the cost of maintaining motivation.

8.5 Darwin Refutes the Libertarians

The issues that Darwinian competition throws up for the neoclassical and Marxist schools of economics are interesting but what it implies for the libertarian school is positively fascinating. Recall that the libertarian paradigm is one in which the ideal economy will arise out of a social system as close to a natural one as possible. To the libertarians, a world of minimal government interference – with little or no taxation or regulation – is optimal. In this world everyone is free to get on with their own life, free to do the best they can.

It is a lovely story; I certainly found the idea initially appealing. Unfortunately, there is the nagging problem of the experimental data, which somehow just does not chime with the libertarian ideal. Afghanistan and Somalia have got little in the way of government and regulation but they are hardly the utopian power houses of economic progress described by libertarianism. I shall be brave here and boldly state that there is not one example of a successful society run along libertarian principles on earth today. What's more, I can confidently state that there never has been and never will be such a society. The reason for this is the darker side of our Darwinian nature.

A few months ago I saw a wonderful piece of wildlife cinematography; it was also the most eloquent exposition of Darwinian evolution in all its brutal reality. The film crew had recorded a small herd of bison being chased by a pack of wolves across a snow-covered, partially wooded wilderness. The wolves caught the herd of bison and were milling around trying to separate an animal from the pack to attack. Eventually, the herd made a run for it, leaving a few animals behind.

The wolves gave chase to the herd. Presently a smaller, younger animal fell back from the herd. The pack of wolves began attacking it. For a few moments it looked to be touch-and-go as to whether the wolves would be able to bring the young bison down. But then a remarkable thing happened.

One of the larger bulls had been left behind when the herd made their escape and was now galloping back to the herd. Between it and the herd was the younger bison, surrounded by the wolves. Rather than running around the pack of wolves – which, for a fleeing animal, might have appeared the most sensible option – the larger bull charged directly at the younger, beleaguered bison.

The bull's intention was not to scare away the attacking wolves. Rather, as it galloped towards its young relative, it lowered its head – and charged directly into the animal. The young bison was flipped into the air and landed helplessly on its side in the middle of the attacking pack of wolves. In this helpless state, the young bison kept the wolves busy while the older animal made his escape.

The larger bull continued on its way, making it safely back to the herd, and probably went on to pass its DNA onto another generation. The younger animal did not get to pass on its DNA. The older bull had sacrificed its younger relative in order to make good its own escape. This is the darker side of Darwinism and it's a big problem for the libertarian school of economics, which relies on the utopian idea that it is possible to build a society in which individuals will leave each other alone to maximise their own wellbeing.

It does not take much imagination to see what Darwinian competition would do to a libertarian society. For argument's sake, let us imagine we start a society from scratch as a perfect libertarian experiment. We place, say, 100 individual men and women on an isolated tropical island. At the start of the experiment, they are all perfect strangers. For how long would they live as pure individuals? My guess is a little less than five minutes. There would be immediate benefits to forming cooperative groups for all sorts of reasons: to construct shelters, to collect food or firewood for example. The benefits of individuals forming cooperative groups is a foundation stone of Adam Smith's philosophy of economics. You cannot get the benefit of specialisation, through the division of labour, without working in groups.

Now let's make the experiment a little more realistic in the Malthusian sense. Let us say the island is only large enough to feed 90 people (alternatively we could just wait until the original 100 bred until the island could not support the population). At this point there is now an incentive to form alliances for defensive reasons, to protect food stores, and to protect territory. Even once those groups have formed there is still going to be a shortage of food and therefore a tangible evolutionary incentive to become the leaders of those groups.

The initial condition of 100 individuals would be a highly unstable state. The Darwinian instinct for survival would immediately cause the 100 to self-organise into a tribal system, and the tribal system to establish a leadership structure. Once the initial pecking-order was established, the Darwinian incentive of the group's leaders would be very much focused on making sure they retained their positions at the top of the freshly formed tribal system.

Over time, the elites of these tribal groups would seek to develop laws and customs, ownership rights and taxation systems that enshrine their position at the head of the group. And since we're talking of a Darwinian world here, they would also seek to ensure that their higher social status is passed on to their own offspring if at all possible. This would be a society in which the ruling elite has every incentive to maintain the status-quo. In short, it would be a feudal society, characterised by fixed leadership and rigid social structures. This would not be a society in which entrepreneurial activity – which could disrupt the social order – is encouraged. There would be the occasional revolution as the dispossessed seek to overthrow the leadership, but these changes would make little difference as the incentives facing the new leadership would inevitably be the same as those facing the previous leadership. Overall, it would be feudal society ruled by vested interest and nepotism, far from the rule-free nirvana described by libertarians. Today's libertarians may choose to call such a society a private-sector arrangement, but for those at the bottom of the tribe it would feel very much like they were suffering a large government overhead.

This line of reasoning suggests that if we are Darwinian competitors and there is anything like a natural human economic system, it is something much closer to the feudal model than anything described by the classical, neoclassical, libertarian or Austrian paradigms. In essence this is a model where everyone sprints along the hedonic treadmill and the first one to get to the front then immediately hits the stop button to freeze the social order in place.

This is not an attractive picture but it is a reasonably accurate description of 99.5% of human history. In some areas of the world feudalism is an accurate description of 100% of human history. If you've ever wondered why the rulers of North Korea are happy for their country to remain an impoverished economic backwater, Darwinian self-interest and its consequent feudal model is the explanation. For today's North Korean leader Kim Jong-un, the son of Kim Jong-il the previous leader, who was in turn the son of Kim il-sung the leader before him, everything is arranged in fine Darwinian feudal order.

If we humans are Darwinian competitors, the libertarian utopia can only ever be the briefest of stopovers on the road to serfdom.

To quote economist Robert Frank on this issue: "Many of the libertarians' most cherished beliefs, which are perfectly plausible within Smith's framework, don't survive at all in Darwin's." Frank's book, *The Darwin Economy*, is well worth a read (Frank, 2011).

It is amusing to observe that Marxists and libertarians, who consider themselves to be polar opposites, both take the same unnaturally optimistic view of human nature. The Marxists believe it is possible to persuade us to work for the common good with no prospect of gaining advantage over our neighbours. The libertarians believe we will work only for ourselves, never seeking to gain advantage over our neighbours.

Both the libertarian and Marxist paradigms are hopelessly naïve, and both fail entirely under the scrutiny of Darwin's scientific theory. Marxism inevitably spirals into a repressive and coercive system, while libertarianism evolves into feudalism. If there is a distinction between these two states of the world, it is one so fine as to make no practical difference. If we are Darwinian competitors, any difference between Marxism and libertarianism is, in the long run, likely to prove illusory: both are cleverly disguised feudal systems.

8.6 Summary

The scientific evidence suggests there is good reason to view humans as Darwinian competitors rather than neoclassical optimisers. This paradigm describes almost all of human history very well indeed. But the Darwinian, feudal paradigm, does not describe the part of history that we are really interested in. The last two or three hundred years, give or take a few decades, have been an aberration in the history of mankind. Understanding this wonderful aberration is the purpose of the next chapter.

9 THE PARADIGM SHIFT

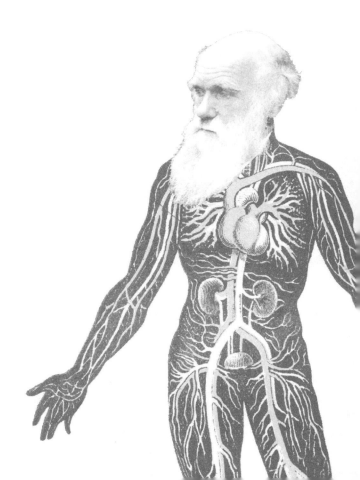

"Each new scientific theory preserves a hard core of the knowledge provided by its predecessor and adds to it."

Thomas Kuhn

I F I HAVE brought you with me up to this point, you should by now be willing to consider that we humans are better modelled as Darwinian competitors than as neoclassical optimisers; that our natural economic system is a stagnant form of feudalism, but this does not explain recent economic progress; that the field of economics is in a confused state of scientific crisis; that scientific revolutions often involve replacing equilibrium models with dynamic circulatory theories; and, finally, that we may need a small shift in perspective and a bit of imagination to push economics beyond its crisis.

The next step is to look for the shift in perspective that simplifies economic theory, explains the origin of economic growth and helps us understand the recent economic malaise. The first step is to ask: What suddenly went right? What changed in our economic system a few hundred years ago to abruptly lift us out of millennia of stagnation into a state of more or less continually improving living standards?

The logical, Spock-like, scientific way to tackle this question is to look at the experimental evidence, asking: When did the economic growth start? Where did the economic growth start? What big event happened at that time and in that place to catalyse economic growth? Equally we should look around the world today and ask ourselves: What differentiates today's most successful economies from the least successful ones?

If we can answer these questions and if the answers point to a common theme then we may have a hint as to what turned on the economic growth machine.

9.1 An Unreasonably Brief Political History of the World

For argument's sake, let's start the political history of humanity, say, 10,000 years ago. As a consequence of our graduating at the top of Darwin's evolutionary training school, we humans acquired two key urges. We acquired the urge to breed more than we could feed, and therefore we also acquired the urge to compete with our neighbours for food and resources. However, we also learnt that we could compete more effectively if we worked in groups. Partly this was due to the productivity advantages arising from the division of labour (as pointed out by Adam Smith) and partly due to safety in numbers. As a result we humans became both competitors and cooperators. We therefore formed tribes.

Within these early tribal societies there was intense Darwinian competition for the leadership roles, as these offered the best breeding and feeding opportunities. Incumbent leaders were, for good Darwinian reasons, strongly motivated to establish hereditary rights and other social structures designed to maintain the status quo, with them at the top of the social order in a position to pass their privileges onto their offspring.

Given the Darwinian urge to breed and the Malthusian shortage of food, competitive pressures inevitably arose between the tribal groups. By sheer weight of numbers, the leadership of larger tribes were inevitably more secure in their positions than those of smaller tribes. Therefore there was an incentive for the leaders of the larger tribes to go on the mergers and acquisitions trail (we still see this effect today in the corporate world). The result of this process was a steady progression toward larger tribes who could establish monopolistic control over large areas of land. For argument's sake, let's call these tribal conglomerates kingdoms.

As the kingdoms became bigger and the wars became bloodier, there was a need for increased administrative sophistication and better weaponry. Kingdoms therefore encouraged the development of writing and some technology. This was by no means a growth-free period. However, as the incumbent elite wanted to remain in place, the preservation of the status quo and social stagnation would have been the prime directive of those at the top.

Given that the evolutionary purpose of being in the leadership positions of these kingdoms was to ensure access to more resources, the natural taxation system would have been regressive. Taxation would have been arranged to maintain a constant flow of wealth upward, from the poor to the rich, for the purpose of supporting the royal court, armies and the inevitably required security apparatus. Occasionally these taxes would become too onerous to bear or the largess of the court too egregious to stomach, in which case the peasantry would become revolting and heads would roll.

This takes care of the first 9,700 years of human political history, a time in which the living standards of humanity improved either not at all or at a pace so slow as to be almost imperceptible. OK – I accept that there were very brief periods when the non-slave populations of the major historical civilisations enjoyed modestly improving living standards; but these successes were transient, and often reversed, so let's not get bogged down in detail.

The second phase of political history began about three and a half centuries ago, in the middle of the 17th century. It began at the same time and in the same place as William Harvey was discovering the circulatory theory of blood and it began with the beheading of one of his favourite patients, King Charles I of England. King Charles I was overthrown and promptly beheaded in 1649, 21 years after Harvey had published his revolutionary theory of blood flow.

This was the period characterised by historians as the start of the enlightenment. Following the Copernican revolution, the zeitgeist of northern Europe was one in which people were, for the first time in well over a millennia, beginning to imagine that things could be done better. Copernicus had shown it was possible to improve on the old order in science and William Harvey had just confirmed it could also be done in medicine. Another, more brutal, revolutionary, Oliver Cromwell (1599–1658), did the same thing with the political structure of England.

Cromwell led the parliamentarians to victory in the English civil war, deposing and beheading Charles I and then turning England into a republic in 1649 – the Commonwealth of England. The English revolution was no sudden shift to what we would call a modern democratic system with universal suffrage. There was pressure for something close to universal male suffrage from a group known as the levellers, but Cromwell had its leaders shot. On the other hand, nor was it a typical feudal revolution involving the simple replacement of one absolute ruler with another. The English revolution was the first faltering step into the second phase of human political history – modern democracy.

Cromwell led the new commonwealth until his death in 1658. Ominously, he was succeeded by his son, Richard Cromwell. But Richard lasted less than a year in his position, after which the son of Charles I was invited back from France to become King Charles II. Charles II ruled from 1660 until 1685 and was succeeded by his brother, James II. Although the monarchy had returned to England after Cromwell's revolution, the democratic genie had been let out of the bottle and parliament was now willing to assert itself more forcefully.

James II lasted only a few years before being deposed in England's next revolution. In 1688, the English parliament invited the Dutch William of Orange and his wife Mary (eldest daughter of Charles I) to invade England, depose James II and take the throne of England. The subsequent invasion and revolution was a near bloodless affair and became known as the Glorious Revolution of 1688.

The English parliament's job offer to William and Mary was generous but it came with significant strings attached in the form of the English Bill of Rights (1689). The Bill of Rights gave the throne to William and Mary but at the same time guaranteed free parliamentary elections, freedom of speech and kept the all-important powers of taxation in the hands of parliament. William and Mary had the throne but parliament kept the power and the mandate to uphold the "indubitable Rights and Liberties of the People of this Kingdom".

All told, the period from 1649 to 1689 was a very odd set of affairs: two kings deposed, a republic formed and then disbanded, an invited invasion and an imported monarch. It was a muddle, but the upshot was an enormous step away from the ancient Darwinian feudal system to one in which there was a concept of equal rights for all. It was a significant milestone on the path to becoming a modern democratic state.

It took almost another century for the next great leap forward towards democracy. The American War of Independence began in 1775. This was quickly followed by the Declaration of Independence (1776),[19] in which the concept of equal rights was again stated forcefully: "all men are created equal, that they are endowed by their Creator with certain unalienable Rights, that among these are Life, Liberty and the pursuit of Happiness."

The American Declaration of Independence then goes on to make an interesting statement: "Governments are instituted among Men, deriving their just powers from the consent of the governed, that whenever any Form of Government becomes destructive of these ends, it is the Right of the People to alter or to abolish it, and to institute new Government."

The American Revolution was followed in short order by the French Revolution (1789–1799). Once again this event was accompanied by a milestone statement of citizens' rights in the form of the Declaration of the Rights of Man. The French statement echoed its American counterpart, the first article stating that men are born and remain free and equal, while the third article declared that sovereignty has its origins in the nation.

---

[19] The American Declaration of Independence was made in 1776, the same year in which Adam Smith published his famous book on economics, *The Wealth of Nations*. It was also around this time that economic progress started to step up a gear. Naturally, economists have been keen to attribute the improvement in economic growth after 1776 to the ideas of Adam Smith, who is after all one of their own (see, for example, the reference made to *The Wealth of Nations* by Alan Greenspan as cited in section 7.1.1.). However, an alternative reading of history is that the improvement in economic growth at this time actually came about more due to the ideas contained in the Declaration of Independence – democracy, to be specific – than those in *The Wealth of Nations*. Since both the Declaration of Independence and *The Wealth of Nations* came about at the same time, the historical record cannot be other than ambiguous on the relative importance of these documents to the change in the pace of economic progress.

In a relatively short space of time the political structures of England, America and France had been decapitated, in England and far more so in France quite literally. What is particularly interesting about these revolutions is that they were not merely the replacement of one feudal ruler with another, as had happened so often through history. The novelty of these revolutions was that they established, for the first time, a circulatory governance structure: "Governments are instituted among Men, deriving their just powers from the consent of the governed." The government was now governed by those it governed.

In summary, political history could be thought of as being divided up into just two distinct periods: the feudal period, characterised by a hierarchical or linear system of government control, and the democratic period, with a circulatory system of control.

It may be just a coincidence that economic progress began to accelerate at around the time of the English, American and French revolutions. It may be just a coincidence that economic progress at that time occurred only in England, America and Western Europe. It may be just a coincidence that when we look around the world today we find that countries with the highest standards of living are overwhelmingly democracies. Then again, maybe it is not a coincidence. Maybe the institutional school of economics is onto something. Maybe democracy, with its circulatory governance structure, is a cause of economic progress.

9.2 A Circulatory Theory of Economic Growth

It is now a fairly straightforward process to arrive at another way of looking at our economic system. All that is necessary is to take the basic Darwinian competitive economic system and marry it with the democratic political system. The result is a surprisingly pleasant combination.

Consider first the basic arrangement of a feudal society. There will be a large number of people with very low incomes and a small number of people with very large incomes (it does not really matter if we talk in terms of income or wealth). As a result the income distribution of the society as a whole could be thought of as a social pyramid, as shown in figure 12.

Figure 12: The income distribution of society represented as a pyramid

The next step is to consider how the private sector and public sector economy would be configured in such a feudal society. This is not difficult to imagine. Given the Darwinian origins of the feudal system the economic arrangements would be configured so as to maintain a constant pressure for wealth to flow upward through the social pyramid toward the top, thereby maintaining the high degree of wealth polarisation desired by the leadership. On the private-sector side, the profits generated by trade, commerce and rental income would tend to favour those at the top of the pyramid. Similarly, on the public side taxation would be configured to support the interests of the ruling elite.

In modern-day language, the tax structure would be configured to be regressive, taking proportionately more from the poor and less from the rich. Therefore in a feudal system both public and private sectors would work together to maintain a polarised income distribution, resulting in a large pool of wealth migrating to the top of the social pyramid. Once at the top of the pyramid this pool of wealth would remain largely stagnant as the ruling elite would have little incentive to do anything with it. Recall that as Darwinian competitors their objective is simply to remain at the top of the pyramid and to keep the whole system in status quo.

This feudal economic configuration, with its flows of wealth, could be represented as shown in figure 13.

Figure 13: A stylised view of the feudal economy

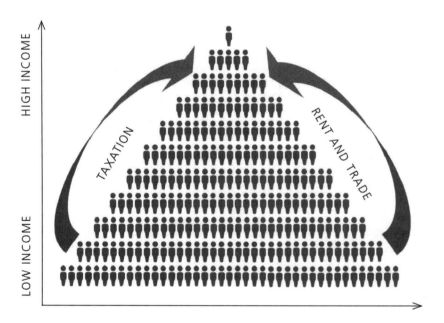

Now consider what would happen once we insert democracy into this system. We know that all three of the English, American and French democratising revolutions were inspired at least in part by the desire for tax reform. It would seem reasonable, therefore, to imagine that adding democracy into the mix would cause a reversal of the direction of flow of the taxation system. The taxation system would be changed from one that was regressive to one that was progressive. That is to say, from one which placed most of the burden on the poor to one that placed proportionately more of the burden on the rich.

This new arrangement, with the direction of the taxation arrow reversed, would now look something like figure 14.

Figure 14: A stylised view of the democratic economy

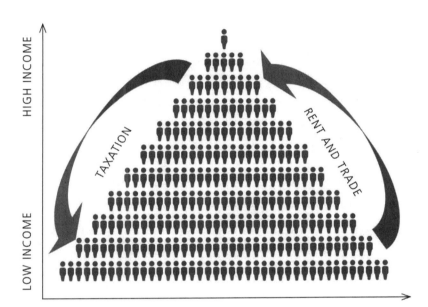

This is where it may be useful to pause for a moment and recall the story of William Harvey and his theory of blood flow. If you remember, before Harvey came along it was Galen's ancient theory of blood flow that dominated medical understanding. In Galen's theory there were two networks transporting blood through the body. The veins carried the dark red venous blood to the body and the arteries carried the bright red arterial blood to the body. Crucially, in Galen's model blood was believed to flow in the *same direction* through both of these systems – both were considered to be blood-distribution systems. In this model the blood did not so much flow as seep slowly through the veins and arteries – it could not flow vigorously because both the venous and arterial systems were in effect dead ends.

We could think of this system as analogous to the feudal economic system, where both the state and private sectors were configured to operate in the same direction, pressing wealth into the dead-end at the top of the social pyramid. In a feudal system, therefore, money and wealth would move only very slowly – in the same way that blood was believed to only flow slowly in Galen's model.

Harvey made just one small change to Galen's model. He reversed the direction of the flow of blood through one leg of the system. In his model, he had the venous system harvesting the blood, which had been distributed through the arterial system, and returning it back to the lungs in order to be re-oxygenated, reinvigorated and then recirculated back to the body. The arterial system became the blood-distribution system and the venous system, its partner, the blood-collection system. In Harvey's new model there were no dead-ends, so the blood could flow vigorously around a single circulatory system.

It does not take a big leap of imagination to think about the reversal of the direction of the flow of taxation, caused by the democratising revolutions, as being similar to shifting from Galen's stagnant dead-end model to Harvey's vigorous circulatory model. This new circulatory flow could be thought of as being generated by the serendipitous partnership between capitalism and democracy. Capitalism would act to push wealth up the social pyramid, while democracy, and its progressive taxation system, would act in the opposite direction to push it back down, causing a vigorous circulatory flow of wealth throughout the economy, as shown in figure 15.

Figure 15: A stylised view of the circulatory flow of wealth through the income pyramid

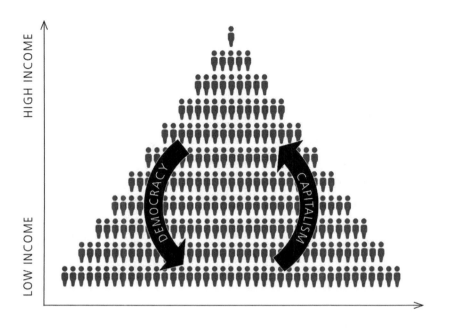

Now consider what this new circulatory flow would mean for the natural Darwinian competitive spirit. Those at the top of the pyramid would no longer be so secure in their position. In the pre-democratic world they would have been confident of being able to sit at the top of the pyramid, collecting their rents, safe in the knowledge that the social and economic arrangements were neatly configured to keep them in situ. In the new democratic world the social arrangements would be less rigid and the debilitating effect of the new progressive tax would be continually undermining their position at the top. The upshot of this reform would therefore be that if you were at the top and you wanted to stay at the top you would suddenly have to compete to do so. Those at the top of the pyramid would have been placed on an invigorating, competitive, hedonic treadmill.

At the bottom of the social order, the Darwinian desire to move higher up the pyramid would also have been enabled by an easing of the social restrictions and a lessening of the tax burden, which might now switch from a headwind to a tailwind as government spending pumps money into the base of the pyramid. This would therefore unleash a significant competitive pressure from the base of the pyramid. In short, the circulatory flow of wealth established by the partnership of democracy and capitalism would have placed the whole social pyramid onto the hedonic treadmill, obliging and enabling everyone to compete to get ahead. Overall, the income or wealth pyramid would remain a pyramid but there would now be a rotation within the pyramid – social mobility – and a dramatic increase in both the money flow and competitive spirit within the economy. The result would be an increase in economic growth generated by none other than the Darwinian competitive pursuit of self-interest as people competed to get ahead of, and stay ahead of, their peers.

The circulatory flow of wealth powering a society-wide hedonic treadmill that in turn generates economic growth could be conceptualised as being similar to Alfred Wegener's idea of continental drift, where subterranean circular convection currents push forward the continental plates. In this circulatory growth model it is the circulatory convection current of wealth generated by the partnership of democracy and capitalism that pushes forward economic growth.

Figure 16: A stylised view of the circulatory flow of wealth driving social mobility, thereby powering the hedonic treadmill

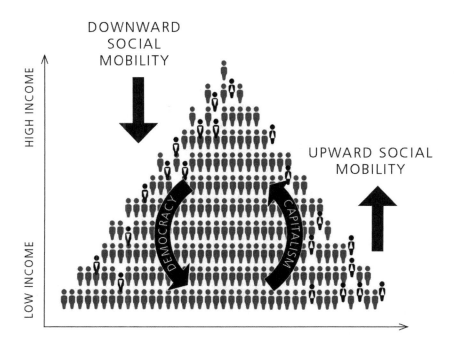

9.3 Resolving the Scientific Crisis in Economics

This simple circulatory model of economic growth goes a considerable way to resolving the state of scientific crisis within economics. A circulatory growth model retains the most important elements of the thinking within the classical school of economics and addresses the most powerful criticisms of capitalism emanating from the left-wing schools of economics, this being the problem of wealth polarisation. At the same time it fully integrates the institutional school and resolves some of the important anomalies thrown up by the behavioural school.

The circulatory model provides a pathway to incorporate the currently neglected issues of economic growth, wealth and income distribution, entrepreneurship and social mobility into the centre of macroeconomic analysis. A circulatory growth model is also a more scientific model than those offered by the mainstream schools of economics in four important respects.

Firstly, it is a model of the whole economy as it stands today, treating both public and private sector activity on an equal footing. Given the comparable sizes of the public and private sectors in a modern developed economy this should be a prerequisite of any reasonable scientific model seeking to describe the real economy.

Secondly, it is a description of the economy as it is now, not a tool of advocacy for persuading policymakers to adopt a different economic system.

Thirdly, it is fully compatible with other fields – namely evolutionary theory.

Fourthly, the circulatory growth perspective passes the empirical test in that it fits broadly with the history of economic growth and with the geographical dispersion of economic success today. That is to say, it explains why economic growth started in Western Europe and North America after their democratising revolutions and failed to start in other areas of the world where strong democracies did not develop.

The circulatory growth model retains the individual pursuit of self-interest as the vital driver of economic growth. In replacing the neoclassical optimisation paradigm with a Darwinian competitive paradigm it even elevates the importance of competition within the economy. The model explicitly recognises the need for income inequality to persist throughout the income distribution in order to maintain growth (this is not strictly necessary in a neoclassical maximisation paradigm). It also makes the maintenance of competitive pressure central to the model. On the other side, the circulatory model recognises that capitalism has a tendency towards wealth and income polarisation and explains how this problem can be, and is in practice, addressed.

In this respect a circulatory growth model can be thought of as a synthesis of many of the most valuable ideas from the apparently irreconcilable right-wing and left-wing schools of economics. It is to be hoped that through integrating the key ideas and concerns of both the traditional right- and left-wings into a single coherent circulatory model it will be possible to achieve a more productive dialogue between these competing philosophies.

These gains do not come for free. There are implications of this model that will likely make people currently on both the left and right of the political spectrum uncomfortable. Those on the right will doubtless find unpalatable the assignment of a positive role for taxation and government spending as a contributor to economic progress. Similarly, those on the left will almost certainly be unhappy with the notion that income inequality is essential for economic growth. Nevertheless, the experimental evidence overwhelmingly supports the conclusion that economic progress is associated with both income inequality and large government.

9.4 A Clear Economic Anatomy

From the perspective of policymakers, one of the most attractive features of the circulatory growth model is that it assigns clearly differentiated, positive functions to both the state and private sectors. At the moment many of those on the right believe that government spending and taxation is always and everywhere an impediment to economic activity. The circulatory growth model suggests a more nuanced perspective on government activity is required.

On the other hand, many on the left who take a dim view of some of the actions of the private sector may also require a more nuanced view of their actions. For example, the tax-minimisation strategies of the private sector have recently come in for significant criticism. When these actions are viewed from a Darwinian competitive perspective it becomes apparent why tax minimisation by the private sector is both inevitable and necessary. If one company were to unilaterally decide not to exploit a legal tax minimisation strategy – a loophole – it would become vulnerable to being either out-competed or taken over by a rival willing to exploit the loophole. In such a situation this decision, however high principled, would have been both damaging and futile. For this reason, those who rail against the private sector for exploiting loopholes may be better advised to target their ire at those responsible for making the rules rather than those who are compelled to exploit them.

The circulatory flow model helps clarify the reality that the agenda of the public and private sectors are both important, both distinct, but also both inevitably in conflict with one another. By openly acknowledging the reality and necessity of this conflict it should be possible for all sides, both public and private, to understand their roles and responsibilities better.

It may be helpful to start thinking of the public and private sectors as something akin to a pair of antagonistic muscles like, for example, the biceps and the triceps. The arm would not work if it had only the biceps or only the triceps. At most it would be able to complete a single operation, after which it would become quite useless. However, with both of the biceps and triceps working together in opposition the combined machine is able to perform repeated work. Both muscles are necessary and yet each hinders the operation of the other. Similarly, in the circulatory growth model the public sector hinders the immediate objectives of private sector – to push wealth up the social pyramid – and the private sector hinders the immediate objectives of the public sector – to push it back down. Yet, taking an enlightened longer-term perspective, it can be seen that the public and private sectors are really working *together* to power the competitive engine of economic progress by maintaining a circulatory flow of wealth.

Recognising and understanding these conflicting agenda should help improve policymaking by giving the state sector better clarity of purpose, allowing it to assess when it should and when it should not bow to the lobbying of the private sector.

9.5 Striking the Balance

If we accept that capitalism and democracy work in creative conflict, as a pair of antagonistic muscles, we can then use the circulatory model to explore what would happen if the strength of these two muscles were to become unbalanced.

Were the government sector to become overly dominant, taxation would rise and entrepreneurial activity would be depressed. As government activity came to dominate the economy entirely, the system would become an essentially Marxist no-growth economy. Conversely, were the democratic side to become too weak and the capitalist side too dominant, one would expect a pooling of wealth at the top of the pyramid – turning the economy into an essentially feudal economy. This would also choke off growth.

This simple thought experiment gives us two no-growth boundary conditions at the points of 0% and 100% government activity. It follows, therefore, that there must be a growth-maximising level of government activity lying somewhere between these zero and 100% boundary conditions, as shown in figure 17.[20]

---

[20] Some readers may be familiar with the similar Laffer curve. According to the argument behind the Laffer curve, a tax rate of 0% will produce no tax revenue and a tax rate of 100% will produce no economic activity – and therefore also no tax for the government. It follows, therefore, that there must be a revenue-maximising level of taxation between 0% and 100%. The logic behind this growth curve is similar.

Figure 17: A representation of the relationship between the government's share of the economy and long-term economic growth

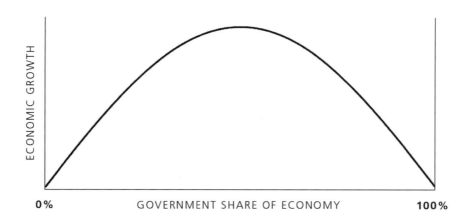

Although imprecise, this curve fits with the broad contours of what we observe in the world today. The most successful economies populate the centre ground, with a balance between state and private sectors. Meanwhile the failed states – Somalia and North Korea, for example – occupy both wings of the distribution, having either clearly too little or too much government.

9.6 Circulatory Growth and Monetary vs Keynesian Policy

Adopting a circulatory growth model can help clarify how we think about a number of important areas of macroeconomic policy. For example, the circulatory model could be used to think about how monetary policies work to stimulate economic growth and how they differ from, say, Keynesian policies.

Broadly speaking, when lending occurs within the private sector it tends to involve transactions running vertically through the wealth pyramid.

Most obviously this is because those at the top of the pyramid are more likely to have the spare money to lend than those lower down. In addition there is also the issue of the interest rates typically charged to those at different positions in the pyramid. Those at the bottom of the social pyramid tend to be seen as having a higher element of credit risk, meaning they are considered more likely to default on a loan, than those higher up the pyramid. For this reason the interest rates charged on loans to poorer people are higher than those charged to wealthy people. For example, in the UK the payday lender Wonga currently charges a representative annual percentage interest rate of 5,853%[21] and generally caters to lower income households (Yes – that really is five thousand eight hundred and fifty-three per cent – it's not a typo!). By contrast, wealthier asset-rich borrowers who, for example, are able to use their home equity as collateral, are able to borrow money for a little under 4% per annum.

Given both the wealth disparities and interest rate disparities running through the social pyramid, it is clearly more rational for those at the top to lend to those at the bottom than the other way round. Of course, in practice this is usually arranged indirectly through institutions, such as banks, which are in turn owned by those at the top. The process of lending money vertically through the social pyramid, at differential interest rates, is one of the principal reasons behind the natural tendency of the private sector to generate a trickle-up effect of wealth flowing from the bottom to the top of the social pyramid.[22]

---

[21] As at September 2013.

[22] This is why all of the world's major religions have, at one time or another, had prohibitions against usury. It is also implicitly acknowledged by the existence of institutions like the US mortgage lender Fannie Mae, the original purpose of which was in effect to counter the tendency for the capital markets to charge unaffordable interest rates to the less well-off. Aside from the obvious trickle-up effect caused by the cost of servicing loans, it is also worth considering the effect of differential interest rates on entrepreneurial activity across the social pyramid. As the economic viability of any given business venture depends on the gap between the return on the capital deployed and the cost of the capital needed to fund the venture, any given venture will be more profitable to those who can secure capital at the lowest interest rates. For this reason it becomes easier for those at the top of the social pyramid, who can borrow at lower rates, to find viable new business ventures than those lower down – I dare say there are very few viable entrepreneurial activities available to those who have to borrow at 5,853%. This effect is part of the innate trickle-up tendency of capitalism which, in the circulatory growth model, is tempered by a progressive taxation system.

Now consider how monetary policy works to generate a quick boost to economic activity. Interest rates are lowered, encouraging a wave of new lending and borrowing. This induces a flow of money – lending – from the top to the bottom of the social pyramid. As this money is then spent, it begins to flow back up the pyramid. In other words, the sudden lending activity stimulates an economically-invigorating boost to the circulatory flow of money around the economy.

However, this debt-fuelled burst of activity is not a free lunch. The legacy of this new borrowing is that the borrower must now send a flow of interest payments back up the pyramid to service the loan and must eventually repay the loan. These interest payments and later principle repayments act in the opposite direction to the original economically-boosting flow of money. Therefore, when the loan is repaid there is the opposite, economically-depressing, circulatory flow – which acts to reduce activity. While the loan is outstanding, and therefore incurring interest charges, it has the effect of strengthening the trickle-up effect of wealth from bottom to top. Given that those at the top of the pyramid tend to spend a lower proportion of their income than those lower down, this also has a depressing effect on overall economic activity.

For this reason, when monetary policy is used to stimulate economic activity by encouraging more private-sector borrowing, it tends to produce an immediate boost to activity followed by a longer-term drag on activity. This is why politicians are often enthusiastic supporters of policies designed to encourage more borrowing immediately before elections but often become less enthusiastic once the election has passed.

To extend the analogy between the circulatory flow of money through the economy and the circulatory flow of blood through the body, the effect of accumulating a large stock of private sector debt is akin to causing economic stenosis – a narrowing of the monetary arteries – which reduces the circulatory flow of money and thereby also reduces economic activity. It is important to understand that the economic stenosis only presents itself when the process of debt accumulation stops – this being the Minsky moment.

Since the start of the 1980s, the central banks of the larger developed countries – led especially by the US Federal Reserve – have used their monetary policies as tools to boost private sector debt levels in order to prevent recessions and to boost expansions. Using a circulatory flow model it becomes easy to understand how this policy leads to greater wealth polarisation, caused by larger interest payments flowing from the bottom to the top of the pyramid, and therefore to weaker long-term economic activity.

At this point, it may be useful to perform a quick thought experiment to help clarify these relationships. Consider a situation in which the level of indebtedness of the bottom half of the pyramid to the top half of the pyramid has risen to the point at which all of the income of the bottom half is paid to the top half as interest payments. In this situation all of the wealth would flow up to the top of the pyramid, the circulatory flow of money through the economy would be entirely choked off and economic activity would stall. In effect, the bottom half of the pyramid would have entered a situation of debt-serfdom to that of the top half. Although only a thought experiment, this helps demonstrate the unfortunate longer-term implication of encouraging ever-higher debt levels through monetary policy and other government policies.

Taking this line of reasoning one step further, once policymakers embark on this path of boosting economic activity through debt accumulation they risk becoming embroiled in a self-perpetuating policy error from which it becomes increasingly difficult to escape. The first wave of policy-induced stimulation leaves a legacy of debt which polarises incomes and depresses future activity. Counteracting this future depressed level of economic activity then requires still further monetary stimulus. Thus the policy of debt-promotion becomes a self-perpetuating autoshambles.

The inevitable end result of this strategy is a highly polarised society with very high debt levels and very low levels of economic growth, which then requires abnormally low interest rates in order to prevent widespread defaults and increasing levels of government spending needed to augment the debilitating effect of the interest payments. This is, of course, exactly the situation hindering many of our economies at the moment.

To be clear, when governments and central banks use their policies to encourage private sector debt accumulation they are increasing the wealth-polarisation process of the private sector, reducing the long-term growth prospects of their economies and driving up their future deficits.

Worryingly, policymakers still do not appear to have grasped the longer-term costs associated with encouraging ever-higher debt levels. Having now exhausted the ability to encourage higher debt levels through cutting central bank interest rates, policymakers have cast around for increasingly exotic debt-boosting strategies. Quantitative easing, forward rate guidance, direct government subsidies of mortgage borrowing and – the most pernicious of all monetarist strategies – the promotion of student debt are all now being deployed as new debt-boosting ruses.

Quantitative easing is by far the most popular of the new wave of exotic monetarist strategies. Around the world central bankers have deployed trillions of dollars in this way. Once again it is easy to use a circulatory growth model to understand why these enormous amounts of money have produced so little real economic growth. Quantitative easing involves the purchase of private sector assets by central banks. Since these transactions involve boosting the money supply – by swapping assets for newly printed money – the monetarist logic of the central bankers leads them to expect this policy to boost economic activity. A circulatory growth model suggests something different. As the holders of the purchased assets are predominantly at the top of the social pyramid, the monetary injection also occurs at the top of the pyramid and therefore at the top of the income distribution. From this position there is little incentive for the private sector to do anything with the new money – it is after all already where they want it to be.

Therefore the money created by the quantitative easing programs sits, largely unused, outside of the circulatory system, as a sort of multi-trillion-dollar monetary haematoma. This is why as quantitative easing programs have pumped up the money supply, the velocity of monetary circulation has collapsed – negating any benefits from the policy.

We can also use the circulatory flow model to consider the operation of Keynesian stimulus policies. Keynesian stimulus works in a slightly different way to monetary stimulus. In the Keynesian approach the government attempts to stimulate the economy by borrowing and then spending money. As the government boosts its spending, it tends to inject the new money predominantly into the base of the social pyramid. Being at the base of the pyramid, there is an automatic incentive for the private sector to compete for this new money in order to turn it into profits and thereby to send it higher up the pyramid. In addition as those at the bottom of the pyramid tend to spend a greater proportion of their income there is also greater propensity to spend the money supplied through Keynesian stimulus rather than the money supplied through monetary stimulus. For this reason, the money added into the system through Keynesian stimulus tends to enter the circulatory system directly, whereas monetary stimulus is effective only if it is also accompanied by both a willingness for those at the top of the pyramid to increase their lending and a willingness for those at the bottom to increase their borrowing. As with the monetary stimulus policies, Keynesianism is also not a free-lunch. The legacy of the government stimulus is also higher levels of debt which must be both serviced and later repaid.

As the debt accumulated by Keynesian stimulus sits on the government's balance sheet it must be serviced and eventually repaid by taxation. As discussed previously, in a modern democratic society, the taxation system tends to be arranged to be progressive. Therefore both the interest payments and principle repayments associated with Keynesian stimulus are, eventually, drawn proportionately more from the top of the social pyramid. Therefore Keynesian policy can be understood as producing a near-term injection of money into the base of the pyramid followed by a delayed withdrawal of money from the middle and top of the pyramid. Seen in this way it is easy to understand how, both through the initial spending and later repayment, Keynesian stimulus tends to act in the same direction as the normal circulatory system. By contrast, monetary stimulus can be thought of as generating an initial, activity-boosting flow that goes in the same direction as the normal circulatory motion, followed by a later, activity-diminishing flow that acts counter to the normal circulatory motion.

Viewed in this way, from the perspective of the circulatory growth model, it becomes possible to understand more intuitively when monetary stimulus is the correct tool to stimulate an economy and when Keynesian stimulus is the better instrument.

In a situation where policymakers are confronted with an otherwise healthy economy which, for whatever reason, has suddenly suffered a negative shock to confidence, monetary stimulus would likely be the ideal tool. In such circumstances, confidence and therefore spending and borrowing might have suddenly fallen, leading to a sharp downshift in economic activity. An abrupt, temporary reduction in interest rates could prove effective in restoring a normal level of borrowing and spending, leading to a restoration of normal economic activity. Once the recovery is in place, the stimulus should then be removed. In other words, it may be useful to think of monetary stimulus as a sort of macroeconomic defibrillator: useful for delivering a short corrective boost in response to an extreme acute problem. If, on the other hand, the economic malaise is the result of a much more structural problem – such as excessive indebtedness – then monetary stimulus may work temporarily but at the cost of compounding the problem in the long run. In this circumstance, Keynesian stimulus is clearly the correct tool to use.

It goes without saying that the preferable course of action is to avoid driving the economy into a situation of excessive indebtedness in the first place. But we must deal with the economic situation as it is today and not the one we would prefer to have. Which brings me to the topic of the next and final chapter, which is concerned with applying the circulatory growth model to the current economic situation and exploring what it says about the correct policy mix needed to restore a more normal level of economic growth.

10 POLICY IMPLICATIONS

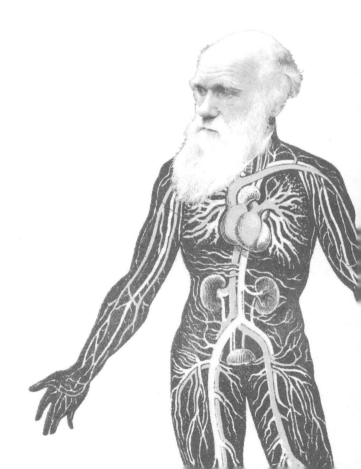

Mr Spock: "It is logical. The needs of the many outweigh…"

Admiral Kirk: "…the needs of the few."

Star Trek II: The Wrath of Kahn (1982)

WE ARE NOW in a position to use the circulatory growth model to help explain both the causes of the global financial crisis and why the policy mix applied after the crisis has failed to restore normal levels of economic growth. We can then use the model to see which policy changes will be necessary in order to help the economy achieve stronger growth.

In this chapter I have chosen to describe developments in the American economy. However, I have chosen to make comments that are relevant to both the American and British economies. Both the American and British economies have followed very similar policies over recent decades, and as a result are now facing the same economic challenges. That said, many of the themes discussed in this chapter are also present, to a greater or lesser degree, in other developed economies.

Figure 18: A time series showing the ratio of all outstanding credit instruments (debt) relative to GDP for the US economy

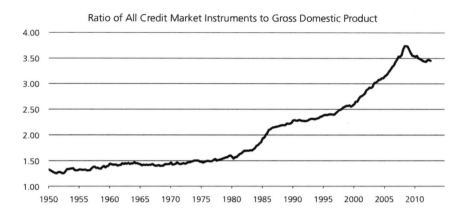

Source: Board of Governors of the Federal Reserve System, U.S. Department of Commerce – Bureau of Economic Analysis

In the mid-1980s the American economy began accumulating debt at a much faster rate than its economy was growing. As a result, the ratio of debt to gross domestic product (a measure of the overall size of the economy) increased dramatically from the mid-1980s until the onset of the global financial crisis in 2007 (figure 18).

The accumulation of debt was facilitated by the deregulation of the financial services industry, beginning in the 1980s, as well as by a trend-decline in global inflationary pressures. Central bankers in the West have been keen to claim the reduction of global inflation as a triumph of their monetary policies, but an alternative explanation is simply that inflation was held in check by price competition from the low-wage developing economies that became major exporters during this period.

As inflation fell, the US Federal Reserve bank and the central banks of other major developed markets progressively reduced interest rates from the mid-1980s onwards (figure 19).

Figure 19: Interest rates began falling at the start of the 1980s

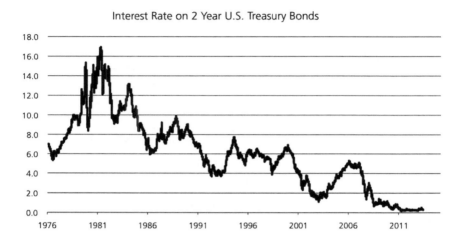

Interest Rate on 2 Year U.S. Treasury Bonds

Source: Board of Governors of the Federal Reserve System

Despite the fact that interest rates fell sharply from the mid-1980s, the pace of debt-accumulation in this period was so rapid that debt-service payments nevertheless rose from around 10% of the disposable household income to a peak of 14% just prior to the onset of the global financial crisis (figure 20). Note that figure 20 shows the household debt service burden in aggregate; it does not show that from the 1980s onwards the incomes of those at the top were rising more rapidly than those at the bottom, while the debt levels were rising more rapidly for those at the bottom than for those at the top. For this reason, figure 20 does not capture the full wealth-polarising effect of the debt-boom shown in figure 18.

Once the global financial crisis hit in 2007, the Federal Reserve cut its base-rate sharply. The lower interest rates, together with a wave of defaults, especially on mortgage debt, brought the debt-service burden of American households back down to around 10% of disposable income.

Figure 20: Household debt-service burden as a percentage of disposable income

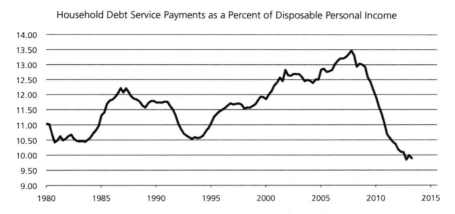

Source: Board of Governors of the Federal Reserve System

As a result of the economic contraction caused by the crisis, the federal government suffered the double whammy of lower tax receipts and higher expenditures, causing the largest deficit since the second world war (figure 21).

Figure 21: US federal government deficit as a percentage of gross domestic product

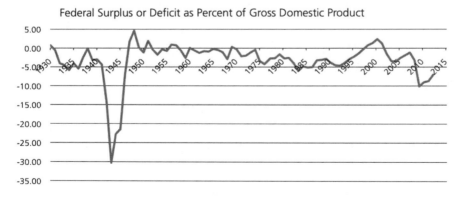

Source: Federal Reserve Bank of St. Louis,
The White House – Office of Management and Budget

The surging federal deficit pushed the ratio of federal debt to GDP up sharply, from just over 60% prior to the crisis to just over 100% (figure 22).

Figure 22: Government debt, as a percentage of GDP, began increasing in the 1980s but really took off after the 2007 crisis

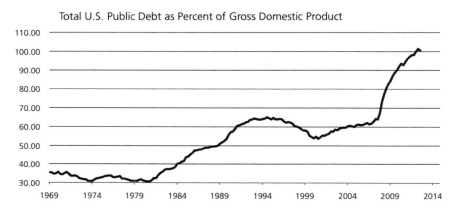

Total U.S. Public Debt as Percent of Gross Domestic Product

**Source: Federal Reserve Bank of St. Louis,
The White House – Office of Management and Budget**

In the mid-1980s the share of GDP taken by corporate profits began increasing from a low level of just over 3% to the current record high of around 11% (figure 23). The trend-increase in corporate profits has been erratic but nevertheless pronounced; it has also coincided with the trend-increase in debt over the same period.[23]

---

[23] Debt accumulation acts to boost profits as it allows corporate revenues to rise faster than expenses. In aggregate, if workers are borrowing money they are able to boost their spending, thereby providing higher revenues to companies without those companies needing to pay higher wages.

Figure 23: Corporate profits have risen to take a record share of GDP

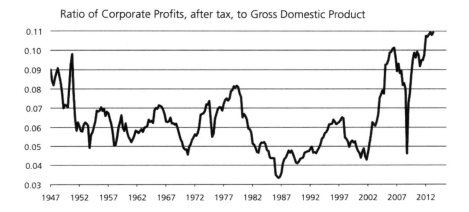

Ratio of Corporate Profits, after tax, to Gross Domestic Product

**Source: Board of Governors of the Federal Reserve System,
U.S. Department of Commerce – Bureau of Economic Analysis**

It is important to note that the ratio of debt to GDP began expanding, corporate profits began rising and income inequality began widening all at the same time. Figure 24 shows the history of the Gini ratio for the United States. The Gini ratio is a measure of income inequality. A Gini ratio of 0 means that there is perfect income equality in society – everyone gets the same income – and a Gini ratio of 1 means that there is perfect inequality – one person gets all of the income. Once again this measure shows a trend change in behaviour which begins in the mid-1980s.

Figure 24: The Gini ratio for the US, showing a trend toward greater income inequality

Gini Ratio For All U.S. Families

Source: U.S. Department of Commerce – Census Bureau

Interestingly, despite the great leveraging process that began in the mid-1980s, the average rate of economic growth of the American economy did not pick up in this period (figure 25). However, the volatility of economic growth was generally lower through the 1980s and 1990s. This decline in economic volatility has been dubbed the "Great Moderation" and was arguably achieved because during this period the Federal Reserve operated monetary policy in a 'risk management paradigm' to smooth out any economic downturns. This was achieved by tactically lowering interest rates in order to encourage more borrowing whenever economic activity faltered or was expected to falter. It was therefore a contributor to the debt boom shown in figure 18.[24]

---

[24] At this point I shall inexcusably work in a plug for my earlier book, *The Origin of Financial Crises: Central banks, credit bubbles and the efficient market fallacy* (2008), which discusses monetary policy mistakes in this pre-crisis period.

In the years since the turn of the millennium the rate of economic growth in America has shifted down to a discernibly lower average level of around 2% a year, rather than the more normal 3.5 to 4% growth rate that persisted in earlier decades.

Figure 25: Showing the annual growth rate of GDP in the US

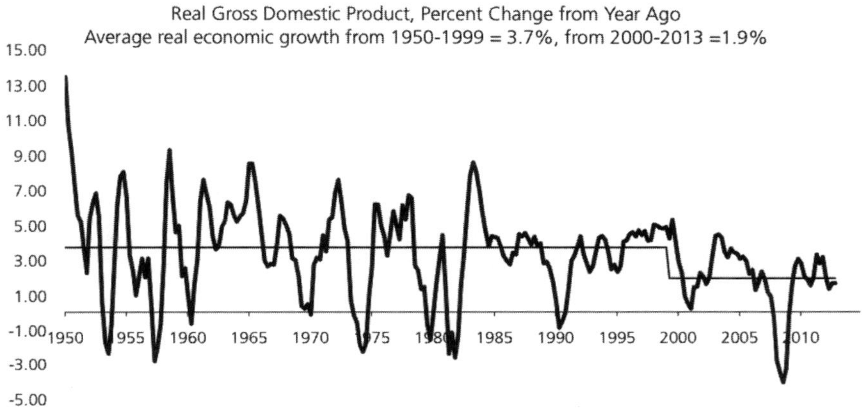
Real Gross Domestic Product, Percent Change from Year Ago
Average real economic growth from 1950-1999 = 3.7%, from 2000-2013 =1.9%
15.00
13.00
11.00
9.00
7.00
5.00
3.00
1.00
-1.00
-3.00
-5.00
1950
1955
1960
1965
1970
1975
1980
1985
1990
1995
2000
2005
2010

Source: U.S. Department of Commerce – Bureau of Economic Analysis

To the layman this modest downshift in the average rate of economic growth since 2000 may appear insignificant, but when this poor growth is considered in the context of the monetary and fiscal stimulus deployed in this period the picture becomes rather more worrying. Since 2007 the very modest level of economic growth has come at the price of a 40% rise in the ratio of federal debt to GDP (figure 22) and a quadrupling of the ratio of the money supply relative to GDP (figure 26). Taken together, figures 22, 25 and 26 paint a very troubling picture. Policymakers are running the monetary pumps at full power in an effort to bail out the economic ship, but the ship continues sitting very low in the water, implying that there must be something very wrong beneath the surface.

Figure 26: The monetary base of the US economy relative to GDP

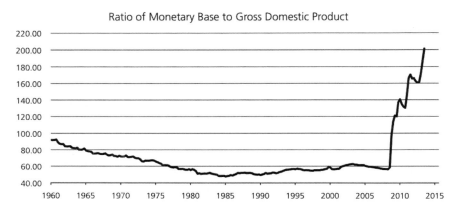

Source: Board of Governors of the Federal Reserve System,
U.S. Department of Commerce – Bureau of Economic Analysis

At the same time that the average growth rate of the American economy moved lower, the velocity of the money in circulation also began to slow (figure 27). Together, figures 26 and 27 show that vast quantities of money are being injected into the American economy but this money is becoming increasingly stagnant – a monetary haematoma.

Figure 27: The velocity of money in circulation within the US economy is at a record low

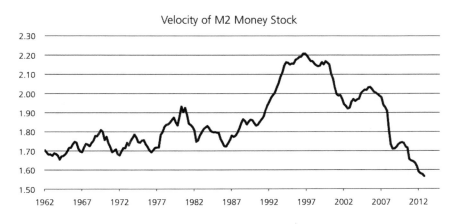

Source: Federal Reserve Bank of St. Louis

Neither the neoclassical school of economics, which dominates academic circles, nor the monetarist school, which dominates policy circles, provides a framework for understanding the interrelationships between these charts.

Neither of these schools has anything at all to say about the rising level of income inequality in American society or the rising level of indebtedness or how these developments may relate to economic growth.

Since government spending is absent from both of the neoclassical and monetarist frameworks, neither school helps us understand the changing fiscal position of the US government or the associated rise in federal debt.

As the neoclassical school largely ignores the role of money in the economy it has nothing to say about the quite remarkable money supply chart (figure 26). By contrast, money supply is of course central to the monetarist school, but developments since 2007 have comprehensively refuted the monetarist paradigm. Despite the enormous increase in the money supply there has been neither the surge in economic activity promised by the monetary optimists nor the surge in inflation threatened by the monetary pessimists (figure 28). The experimental evidence suggests that money supply has rather less effect on economic activity than the monetarists would have us believe. Perhaps as suggested in the earlier discussion of the fictitious freightist school of economics (section 7.1.4), the monetarists have simply misunderstood the direction of causality between economic activity on one side and credit creation and money supply on the other. Strong economic activity drives up credit-creation and the money supply, but strong money supply does not necessarily drive up economic activity. This is especially true once the economy has entered a state of excessive indebtedness.

Figure 28: Despite the surge in money supply, inflation (outside of asset prices) has remained subdued

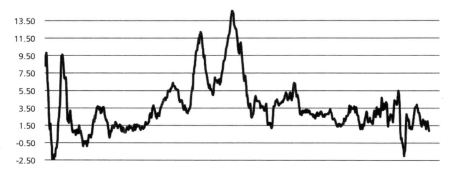

Consumer Price Index for All Urban Consumers, annual percentage change

Source: U.S. Department of Labor – Bureau of Labor Statistics

By contrast, when all of these charts are viewed from the circulatory growth paradigm they fit together like the pieces of a jigsaw puzzle and form a single, simple picture. The rising level of indebtedness since the mid-1980s means that those at the bottom of the social pyramid have become increasingly indebted to those at the top of the pyramid. This indebtedness requires that the bottom of the social pyramid devotes a greater proportion of its income toward debt-service payments, which are made to those higher up. These payments boost corporate profits (much of the surge in corporate profits has come from financial services) and ultimately this drives the Gini ratio higher.

For as long as those at the top of the pyramid were willing to increase their lending to those lower down – and those lower down were also willing to increase their borrowing from those higher up – the upward flow of interest payments could be recirculated back down the pyramid, in the form of new loans, to generate new spending. In this way the circulatory flow and therefore economic activity was sustained, but only at the cost of ever rising indebtedness – in short, a macroeconomic Ponzi scheme.

When the global financial crisis hit in 2007, the lending and spending binge came to a halt as both sides realised that the debt burden could no longer be serviced. Those at the bottom lost their appetite to borrow and those at the top lost their appetite to lend. The circulatory flow was broken, or at least severely curtailed, causing a sharp decline in economic activity. At this point the government was required to step in to artificially complete the circuit with deficit spending and yet more monetary stimulus. In this way it is possible to understand that today's unpleasant combination of low growth despite large government deficits – a condition recently dubbed 'secular stagnation' – is the direct and inevitable consequence of the debt bubble, which is itself largely due to previous excessively easy monetary policy.

After the crisis, the Federal Reserve cut its base rate to essentially zero but, due to the debt overhang, this was insufficient to reignite the borrowing binge. At this point a second tactic was deployed. Quantitative easing programmes were initiated whereby the Federal Reserve purchased bonds from the private sector. This gave the private sector more money (figure 26) in the hope and expectation that this money would then generate economic activity.

Since the bonds purchased as part of these quantitative easing programmes were held predominantly by those at the top of the social pyramid, the monetary injection (transfusion) also occurred into the top of the social pyramid. However, with the financial situation of those at the bottom of the pyramid remaining precarious, there was little incentive for those at the top to lend them this new money. As a result, this new money mostly stagnated within the banking system (figure 27) where it remains on deposit or leaks out into asset-price inflation without generating meaningful economic activity. In short, quantitative easing simply puts the money into the wrong position within the circulatory system. Had the money been injected into the base of the pyramid there would have been a tremendous incentive for the private sector to leap into action in order to compete to turn this new money into revenues and then profits.

Looking at these charts from a more abstract perspective, the story they tell is one in which the rising level of indebtedness of the US economy is strengthening the natural tendency of the private sector to cause wealth to trickle-up the social pyramid, thereby weakening the growth-generating circulatory flow of wealth through the economy. Put differently, the debt-boom has strengthened the private-sector biceps without doing the same for the state-sector triceps. For this reason the accumulation of private-sector debts leads first to higher deficit spending and then, if uncorrected, either to permanent economic stagnation or higher taxation.

At the risk of painting an overly emotive picture, the heightened debt-load of the American economy is incrementally restoring an economic system that looks increasingly like the pre-revolutionary, stagnant, feudal model where those at the top of the social order can continue moving ever further ahead of those lower down by virtue of the income generated by interest and rents alone. It is perhaps understandable that the term *debt-serfdom* has emerged recently as a description of this new economic configuration.

At present this unhealthy economic configuration is being kept on life-support by a combination of unsustainable deficit-spending and increasingly futile monetary policies. The short-term modest success of these policies, in restoring economic stability after the global financial crisis, should not be misinterpreted as having put the economic system back onto a sustainable growth path.

Fortunately, once the diagnosis of the disease becomes clear, so too does the necessary course of treatment.

10.1 The Fifth Labour of Hercules

According to Greek mythology, Hercules was ordered to perform 12 labours as penance for having killed his six sons in a fit of insanity. The fifth of these labours was to clean the legendary Augean stables. The story goes that these stables housed an enormous herd of abnormally healthy animals and had not been cleaned for over 30 years.

Hercules declared that he would perform the seemingly impossible task of cleaning the stables in a single day in return for a payment of 10% of the herd of cattle. King Augeas agreed to this bargain.

Naturally, Hercules successfully cleaned the stables in a day, without getting his hands dirty – it would hardly be the stuff of legend otherwise. Hercules's trick was simplicity itself. He diverted the course of two nearby rivers, the Alpheus and the Peneus, so that they would both flow through the stables and flush the problem away.

The problems confronting Hercules in cleaning up the stables and those confronting ourselves in cleaning up our economies are similar. Hercules was faced with a pile of dung that had taken 30 years to accumulate; we are faced with an analogous pile of debt that has also taken 30 years to accumulate. Hercules achieved his task by diverting two rivers; we can do the same by diverting two monetary flows. Unfortunately, there the similarity ends – our task is not going to be completed in a day, nor without getting our hands dirty.

10.1.1 First: stop the herd from adding to the problem

Hercules would have first needed to get the animals out of the Augean stables in order to prevent them from adding to his problem. Similarly, our first line of attack should be to identify the government policies specifically designed to promote the further accumulation of debt and stop those policies.

One source of new borrowing that looks especially dangerous from the circulatory growth perspective is the recent dramatic rise in student debt. According to the Federal Reserve's monthly Consumer Credit Report, the stock of student loans in America has moved from $731 billion in 2008 to an estimated $1.214 trillion in Q3 of 2013 – a 66% increase in less than five years. By comparison, motor vehicle loans moved from $777 billion to $861 billion over the same period – an 11% increase.

Figure 29: In the US, student debt is rising rapidly

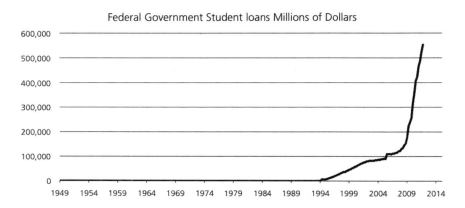

Source: Board of Governors of the Federal Reserve System

The accumulation of student debt, and the associated inflation of tuition fees it appears to be facilitating, looks especially troubling when viewed from a circulatory-growth perspective.

In the first instance, the repayment of student debt acts rather like the imposition of a higher marginal tax rate upon fresh graduates. This makes the taxation system less progressive, which thereby weakens the growth-generating circulatory flow. What's more, this higher marginal tax rate will hit young graduates at a key time, when they are attempting to start careers and families and are also trying to get onto the housing ladder.

Secondly, the prospect of incurring such high debts as part of the education process can only act as a deterrent to those already at the bottom of the social pyramid from entering the education system. For this reason it is likely that the rapidly rising cost of tuition will have a long-term dampening effect on social mobility and associated competitive forces within the economy.

It is not unreasonable to say that each dollar of student debt therefore buys at least two dollars of damage to the circulatory-growth engine.

If one accepts the premise of the circulatory growth model – that a degree of wealth recirculation is required to power the hedonic treadmill – then it becomes very difficult to identify any channel for that recirculation that offers greater economic benefits than the provision of education throughout society. A recent study by the Federal Reserve Bank of St. Louis on the impact of this increase in student debt ends with the following salutary observation:

> "our findings begin to raise questions, but are not definitive, about whether our higher education system, which increasingly relies on student loans to finance college, can retain its position as one of the greatest equalising forces in the American economy."
> (Elliott et al., 2013)

We should be thinking long and hard about the wisdom and future costs of using education as a device to entrap our own children in a position of debt-serfdom. Given the tremendous efficiencies in the dissemination of knowledge permitted by the information revolution, it seems truly perverse that education should suddenly be getting more not less expensive. It may be that university tuition fees are one of those costs that will always expand to consume the amount of money available. If so, a regulatory response is required. If governments abdicate this responsibly and instead act only to facilitate tuition fee inflation via the underwriting of student loans, universities may simply respond with a cycle of ever-higher fees, requiring the provision of ever-greater volumes of student loans – in short, another autoshambles, with worrying social implications.

Moving briefly to the British economy, where another recently introduced policy also looks especially unhelpful – the 'Help to Buy' scheme. Under this scheme the British government lends homebuyers up to 20% of the purchase price of a house valued at £600,000 or less. Officially the idea is to help people get on the housing ladder. Doubtless this policy will have a politically expedient short-term palliative effect on the economy; however, its longer-term side effects may be far from benign.

If houses were abnormally cheap and interest rates abnormally high, such a policy might make macroeconomic sense. In the aftermath of the Great

Depression, the American government established agencies – the Federal National Mortgage Association, more usually known as Fannie Mae – for the purpose of helping the flow of credit to lower-income homebuyers. When established, it was a well-targeted scheme for the prevailing economically depressed conditions. Where the scheme went wrong was in that it was not curtailed once the housing boom of the 1990s turned into the full-blown bubble of the noughties. Fannie Mae continued lending, at breakneck speed, through the housing bubble, and thereby helped create the mortgage credit bubble – the root cause of today's economic malaise. In other words, Fannie Mae managed to perform the dual role of helping cure the Great Depression while also helping cause the Great Recession.

The provision of credit by the government for the purpose of supporting mortgage lending can be a valuable tool, but its efficacy is crucially dependent upon the prevailing economic conditions. With house prices in the UK already elevated, debt levels high, and interest rates abnormally low it is not obviously the wisest course of action for a government to encourage still more borrowing and higher house prices. All things considered, a wiser course of action would appear to be to direct the monies from this scheme toward supporting higher housing supply rather than higher demand – those struggling to get onto the housing ladder would be better served by lower house prices than by larger mortgages.

It is worth considering the very obvious long-term tension between higher tuition fees – something the British government is also promoting – and the Help-To-Buy scheme. As students begin emerging from universities already burdened by high levels of student debt, they will be confronted with an artificially inflated housing market and the need to begin repaying student loans. It may therefore become necessary for the government to provide ever more state aid to help each subsequent generation of graduates get onto the housing ladder. Promoting student debt *and* state mortgage subsidies looks to be two policies at odds with one another, something that could easily evolve into another self-perpetuating autoshambles.

Contrary to popular belief, the phrase 'first do no harm' is not actually part of the Hippocratic oath – but it would make an excellent oath for everyone involved in macroeconomic policy, and especially monetary policy. The first line of attack in restoring our over-indebted economies to balance should be to reconsider all areas of policy that may be inadvertently promoting unnecessarily high levels of borrowing.

10.1.2 Second: change the course of the monetary river

From a circulatory-growth perspective, the process of quantitative easing over extended periods looks to lie somewhere between pointless and damaging. If it is successful in generating a further increase in the level of indebtedness of the economy, it will almost certainly prove counterproductive.

For asset-holders who sell their assets as part of the quantitative easing programme, the mechanism achieves no more than an exchange of one asset – bonds – for another – cash. If this exchange is conducted at a fair price there is no net increase private-sector wealth. In this case the policy is likely to be economically neutral – or in less polite terms, futile. On the other hand, if these purchases of assets act to push up asset prices to a level higher than where they would otherwise trade, the holders of those assets may be considered to have benefitted from a capital gain relative to what they would otherwise have achieved. That is to say if, through quantitative easing, the central bank overpays for the assets it purchases, then it can engineer a wealth transfer from the public to the private sector – by, for example, paying say $110 dollars for a bond that is really worth $100. Such a wealth transfer from public to private sector may be economically justifiable in certain circumstances. That said, as with all such interventions, the crucial thing to consider is the current configuration of the economy when the policy is implemented.

Given that the holders of the assets being purchased are, almost by definition, predominantly at the top of the social pyramid, any benefit of overpayment by the central banks amounts to a transfer of wealth from the state sector to the wealthiest members of the private sector. Since this wealth transfer must eventually be recouped through taxation – which, despite being progressive, is drawn broadly from across the pyramid – the overall effect is to transfer wealth up towards the top of the pyramid from the centre. That is to say, it has the effect of producing a circulatory flow of wealth that runs in the opposite direction to that required by the circulatory growth model. Put bluntly, long-term quantitative easing drives economic growth *down* not up.

Given that stock markets are doing rather well, the Gini ratio is at an all-time high and the velocity of money is suggesting that the wealthy can find little useful purpose for these government handouts, it is not obviously a sensible course of action to continue directing government subsidies to the top of the social pyramid. On balance, quantitative easing – as a long-term strategy to boost economic activity – was always wrongheaded, and is almost certainly now doing more harm than good.

Both monetary and Keynesian stimulus policies have been grossly overused in recent decades. Nevertheless we must deal with the legacy of previous policy mistakes and seek the best strategy from the current economic configuration. The legacy of previous monetary stimulus remains with us in the form of an enormous debt overhang. From this situation it would be folly to attempt a cold-turkey policy of abruptly withdrawing government stimulus. Instead what is needed is a redirection of this stimulus.

The flow of money emanating from central banks needs to be rerouted from the top to the bottom of the social pyramid. That is to say, central banks should stop buying private sector assets and instead start buying bonds to fund infrastructure investment projects that generate employment (figure 31 shows that there are plenty of people to employ). In other words, we need to shift from monetary stimulus towards Keynesian stimulus.

As this Keynesian stimulus is likely to prove more potent than the existing quantitative easing programmes, rather less of it should be required. Nevertheless, again given the precarious starting position, it would be wisest to start with a large Keynesian stimulus and then slim it down over time.

Once again a useful analogy can be drawn between the circulatory systems of blood and money. In the blood system the most invigorating, life-giving blood is the freshly oxygenated blood that emerges from the lungs. In the monetary system, the most invigorating, economically-boosting money is that found at the bottom of the social pyramid, where it is most likely to be spent. Viewed in this way, Keynesian stimulus injects oxygenated money into the economy while quantitative easing injects much-less-useful deoxygenated money.

10.1.3 Third: change the course of the fiscal river

Finally, the unpalatable but unavoidable topic of taxation. Once again it is important to consider the current configuration of the economy. In summary, this configuration has the following characteristics: employment levels are low, wage growth has been lacklustre for a long time (figure 30), levels of indebtedness are high, wealth polarisation is high, corporate profits are very high, as are capital gains. Taking all of these factors together, the message from the circulatory growth model is straightforward: the balance between the taxation of labour and the taxation of capital needs to change toward a lower level of taxation on labour and a higher level of taxation on capital. Specifically, this means higher taxes on capital gains, corporate profits and the earnings from both interest and rents, and lower levels of income tax.

Figure 30: Real wages have been falling in America for over a decade

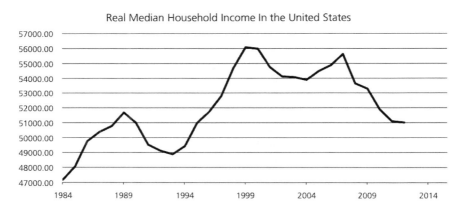

Source: U.S. Department of Commerce – Census Bureau

The traditional argument against such reforms is that they act as a disincentive to investment and will therefore cause entrepreneurs to go on strike. Who better to comment on that particular concern than Warren Buffett: "Let's forget about the rich and ultra-rich going on strike and stuffing their ample funds under their mattresses if – gasp – capital gains rates and ordinary income rates are increased. The ultra-rich, including me, will forever pursue investment opportunities."
(Buffett, Nov 25 2012).

By contrast, the alternative argument that high taxation on wages may be a disincentive for workers is almost never made. However, when one looks at either the employment-to-population ratio (figure 31) or the labour market participation rate (figure 32) there appears to be good reason to worry that it is the ordinary workers that are the ones being disincentivised.

Figure 31: The employment-to-population ratio has not recovered after the crisis

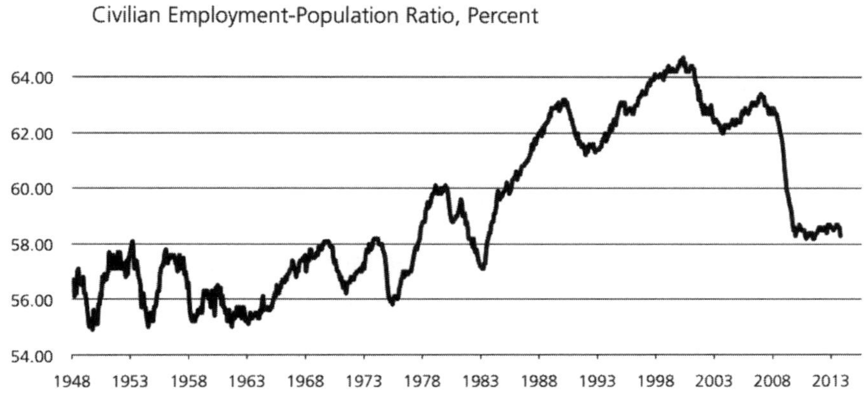

Civilian Employment-Population Ratio, Percent

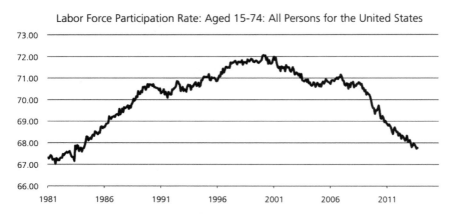

Source: U.S. Department of Labor – Bureau of Labor Statistics

To return to the earlier analogy of the circulatory growth model powering a society-wide hedonic treadmill, it may be fair to say that, at the moment, the treadmill is running a little too slowly at the top of the pyramid and a little too fast at the bottom. Those at the top could do with getting into better shape while those at the bottom are looking exhausted.

Figure 32: Since 2000 the labour market participation rate has been steadily falling

Labor Force Participation Rate: Aged 15-74: All Persons for the United States

Source: Organisation for Economic Co-operation and Development

In summary, the circulatory growth model suggests a three-pronged approach to dealing with the current secular stagnation:

1. Stop the policies designed to promote further private-sector debt-accumulation.

2. Shift from monetary to Keynesian stimulus.

3. Rebalance the burden of taxation between labour and capital – less tax on labour, more tax on capital.

Taken together this combination of policies should inject a considerable new flow of spending into the circulatory system, at the bottom of the social pyramid, thereby triggering a burst of competitive activity from the top of the pyramid. Over time it should also allow and encourage a gradual deleveraging of the economy, bringing it back towards a more balanced situation. Once that deleveraging process has occurred, the wealth-polarising force within the private sector should have been reduced, leading to a contemporaneous reduction in the need for either deficit spending or higher taxation.

In the long run the policy mix should seek to deleverage the economy into a situation in which the normal circulatory growth engine can sustain activity without the need for either monetary or Keynesian stimulus. However, if policymakers choose the easy option of simply adding Keynesian stimulus on top of the existing policy mix *without* encouraging a deleveraging process and *without* rebalancing the burden of taxation, then the imbalances in the economy will likely accumulate and the subsequent crash will be even larger.

10.2 Conclusion

The methodology of neoclassical economics is built on the idea that an economy can be understood as an aggregate of independent, optimising individuals. This approach precludes considering group behaviour, including competitive behaviour. It largely ignores the half of the economy that is controlled by the government and entirely neglects the institutional arrangements of our economy. It also entirely fails to explain why some economies are successful and others are not. It has no mechanism for analysing the role of debt within the economy. It therefore fails to provide a scientific framework for understanding the current economic predicament.

This is not a reasonable state of affairs for a field seeking to describe our economic system scientifically. There may be a better economic system available than the one we have, but the job of economics as a science is first to understand and describe the one we've got. This cannot be achieved by building abstract models of imaginary alternate economies, where governments are absent, markets are perfect and people act as machines rather than humans.

The multiple competing and conflicting schools of economic thought, the apparently irreconcilable disagreements between leading economists, their conflicting theories and their opposing policy advice should be causing alarm bells to ring over the state of the 'science' of economics. That said, there is considerable room for optimism. If economics is indeed in a state of scientific crisis, of the type described by Thomas Kuhn, then it should be possible to find a way out of the crisis. If we are willing to look at the problem from Kuhn's perspective, apply a few of the tricks that have helped turn other fields into true sciences, and be brave enough to imagine things differently, we may find our economies suddenly become both more comprehensible and much easier to manage.

The paradigm shift I have suggested involves thinking of economic growth as being generated by a circulatory flow of wealth through society. In this model, wealth is moved up through the social pyramid by the activity of the private sector and is then recirculated back downward via the activity of the state sector. Viewed in this way, it becomes possible to reconcile the apparently conflicting agendas of the state and private sectors. The state and private sectors are indeed antagonistic to one another but it is a *creative* antagonism and this antagonism is necessary to power the hedonic treadmill which, in turn, is responsible for generating economic growth. Like the biceps and the triceps, neither the state nor private sector can operate usefully without being both in balance and in opposition with one another.

I do not think there is any individual element of this model that can be considered controversial, or which has not been widely discussed for years. However, it is a different methodology to that currently being promoted by mainstream economics and it leads to quite different conclusions on how the economy works and how an optimal economy should be configured.

With democratic capitalism we have inadvertently stumbled upon a system that lets us exploit the best of our competitive nature while managing the worst of our selfish nature. We should celebrate this triumph. We should also be mindful of the need to maintain the balance between the state and private sectors, recognising that this balance is not the natural state of affairs. Due to our innate Darwinian nature, there will always be those seeking to unbalance the system in their favour.

In the spirit of the circulatory theme of this book, I shall end with the extended version of the same quotation I used at the start of the book. The passage comes from Francis Bacon's essay 'Of Seditions And Troubles', and shows that there really never is anything to say in economics that has not already been said. Francis Bacon may be no William Shakespeare, but he had a good turn of phrase and a fair instinct for economics.

"Above all things, good policy is to be used, that the treasure and moneys, in a state, be not gathered into few hands. For otherwise a state may have a great stock, and yet starve. And money is like muck, not good except it be spread. This is done, chiefly by suppressing, or at least keeping a strait hand, upon the devouring trades of usury."

Francis Bacon

BIBLIOGRAPHY

Arnsperger, C., Varoufakis, Y. (2006). 'What Is Neoclassical Economics?', *Panoeconomicus*, 53, no. 1: 5–18 (Belgrade)

Bacon, F. (1625). 'Of Seditions and Troubles', *Essays* (London)

Bernanke, B. (2004). 'The Great Moderation', Meeting of the Eastern Economic Association (Washington DC)

Blanchard, O. J. (2008). 'The State of Macro', *Massachusetts Institute of Technology Department of Economics Working Paper Series*: 08–17 (Cambridge, Massachusetts)

Buffett, W. (25 November 2012). 'A Minimum Tax for the Wealthy', *New York Times* (New York)

Chambers, R. (1844). *Vestiges of the Natural History of Creation* (John Churchill, London)

Cooper, G. (2008). *The Origin of Financial Crises: Central banks, credit bubbles and the efficient market fallacy* (Harriman House, Petersfield)

Darwin, C. (1859). *On The Origin of Species by Means of Natural Selection, or the Preservation of Favoured Races in the Struggle for Life* (John Murray, London)

Desmond, A., Moore, J. (1991). *Darwin: The Life of a Tormented Evolutionist* (Michael Joseph, London)

Elliott, W., Nam, I. (2013). 'Is Student Debt Jeopardizing the Short-Term Financial Health of U.S. Households?', *Federal Reserve Bank of St. Louis Review* (St Louis)

Ernst Fehr, S. G. (2000). 'Cooperation and Punishment in Public Goods Experiments', *American Economic Review*, 90, no. 4: 980–994 (Pittsburgh)

Hayek, F. A. (1944). *The Road To Serfdom* (Routledge Press, London)

Federal Reserve (September 2013). Consumer Credit Release, G 19 (Washington DC)

Fisher, I. (1933). 'The Debt-Deflation Theory of Great Depressions', *Econometrica*, 1, no. 4: 338–357 (New York)

Frank, R. H. (2011). *The Darwin Economy: Liberty, Competition and the Common Good* (Princeton University Press, Princeton)

Friedman, M. (1962). 'The Relation Between Economic Freedom and Political Freedom' , in Boaz, D. (ed.) (1997), *The Libertarian Reader: Classic and Contemporary Readings from Lao-Tzu to Milton Friedman*: 292 (The Free Press, New York)

Greenspan, A. (2005). Remarks by Chairman Alan Greenspan at the Adam Smith Memorial Lecture (Kirkcaldy, Scotland)

Gregory, A. (2001). *Harvey's Heart: The Discovery of Blood Circulation* (Icon Books, Cambridge)

Herndon, T., Ash, M., Pollin, R. (2013). 'Does High Public Debt Consistently Stifle Economic Growth? A Critique of Reinhart and Rogoff', Political Economy Research Institute (University of Massachusetts Amherst)

Keynes, J. M. (1926). *The End of Laissez-Faire* (Hogarth Press, London)

Keynes, J. M. (1936). *The General Theory of Employment, Interest and Money* (Palgrave, London)

Kocherlakota, N. (2010). 'Modern Macroeconomic Models as Tools for Economic Policy', *Banking and Policy Issues Magazine*, Federal Reserve Bank of Minneapolis (Minneapolis)

Krugman, P. (6 September 2009). 'How Did Economists Get it so Wrong?', *New York Times* (New York)

Krugman, P. (18 April 2013). 'The Excel Depression', *New York Times* (New York)

Kuhn, T. S. (1957). *The Copernican Revolution: Planetary Astronomy in the Development of Western Thought*, Harvard University Press (Cambridge, Massachusetts)

Kuhn, T. S. (1962). *The Structure of Scientific Revolutions* (University of Chicago Press, Chicago)

Lazear, E. (2000). 'Economic Imperialism', *The Quarterly Journal of Economics*, 115, no. 1: 99–146 (Cambridge, Massachusetts)

Lenin, V. I. (1913). 'The Three Sources and Three Components of Marxism', in Wishart, L. A. (ed.) (1970), *Karl Marx and Frederick Engels: Selected Works in One Volume*: 23–27 (Lawrence & Wishart, London)

Halperin, M., Siegle, J. T., Weinstein, M. M. (2004). *The Democracy Advantage: How Democracies Promote Prosperity and Peace* (Routledge, London)

Marx, K. (1867). *Capital: Critique of Political Economy*, 1 (Verlag von Otto Meisner, Hamburg)

Minsky, H. P. (1986). *Stabilizing an Unstable Economy* (Yale University Press, New Haven)

Murray, C. (2012). *Coming Apart: The State of White America, 1960–2010* (Random House, New York)

Nietzsche, F. (1889). *Twilight of the Idols, or, How to Philosophize with a Hammer* (Leipzig)

Oreskes, N. (1999). *The Rejection of Continental Drift: Theory and Method in American Earth Science* (Oxford University Press, New York)

Piketty, T., Saez, E. (2012). 'Top Incomes and the Great Recession: Recent Evolutions and Policy Implications', 13th Jacques Polak Annual Research Conference (Washington DC)

Reinhart, C., Rogoff, K. (2009). *This Time Is Different: Eight Centuries of Financial Folly* (Princeton University Press, Princeton)

Repcheck, J. (2009). *Copernicus' Secret: How the Scientific Revolution Began* (JR Books, London)

Saez, E. (2013). 'Striking it Richer: The Evolution of Top Incomes in the United States' (updated with 2012 preliminary estimates), (UC Berkeley)

Siegle, J. T., Weinstein, M. M., Halperin, M. H. (2004). 'Why Democracies Excel', *Foreign Affairs* (New York)

Skousen, M. (2005). *Vienna & Chicago: Freinds or Foes?: A Tale of Two Schools of Free-Market* (Capital Press)

Smith, A. (1776). *An Inquiry Into the Nature and Causes of the Wealth of Nations* (W. Strahan and T. Cadell, London)

Smith, D. (1987). *The Rise and Fall of Monetarism: The theory and politics of an economic experiment* (Penguin, London)

Stigler, G. J. (1976). 'The Successes and Failures of Professor Smith', *Journal of Political Economy*, 84, no. 6: 1199–1212 (University of Chicago Press, Chicago)

Stiglitz, J. E. (2012). *The Price of Inequality: How Today's Divided Society Endangers Our Future* (W. W. Norton, New York)

Syed, M. (2010). *Bounce: Mozart Federer, Picasso, Beckham, and the Science of Success* (Harper, New York)

Veblen, T. (1898). 'Why is Economics Not an Evolutionary Science?', *Quarterly Journal of Economics*, 12, no. 4: 373–397 (Cambridge, Massachusetts)

Wood, R. M. (1985). *The Dark Side of the Earth* (HarperCollins, London)

Wright, T. (2012). *Circulation: William Harvey's Revolutionary Idea* (Chatto & Windus, London)

INDEX

complexifying force 61

conceptual efficiency 33, 44, 121

consumers 116

continental drift 73-5

cooling custard model 72

cooperative behaviour 128, 136, 144

Copernican revolution 10, 19-20,
29-30, 33, 37, 38-42, 43, 145

Copernican Revolution, The 39

Copernicus xv, 29, 37, 38-9, 44, 96

heliocentric model 40-1, 42

Coriolanus 55-6

creationists 59-61

creative

conflict 159

destruction 90

Cromwell, Richard 146

Cromwell, Oliver 145-6

Crosse, Andrew 61

Curie, Marie and Pierre 75

D

Dark Side of the Earth, The 71

Darwin, Charles 10-11, 59, 62-3, 66,
69, 125

Darwinian competition 128-9, 134,
135-6, 137-8, 139

circulatory growth theory and
156

vs libertarians 134-8

vs Marxism 133-4

vs neoclassical school 133

Darwin Economy, The 138

de Lamarck, Jean-Baptiste 61-2

Declaration of Independence (1776)
147

Declaration of the Rights of Man
147

debt 4, 9

accumulation 171-3

-inflation cycle 104

relative to GDP for US
economy 170

-serfdom 163, 181, 184

-service burden 171-2

student 164, 182-3

*Debt-Deflation Theory of Great
Depressions, The* 97-9

deferent 35

democracy 146-7, 148, 151

Democracy Advantage, The 117

deregulation 86

division of labour 63, 136, 144

E

economic

activity 5, 86, 88, 92, 100, 162,
166, 178

growth 12, 166, 176-7, 187

Economic Imperialism 81

economic plane 91-2, 95, 105, 111,
118

economics

fractal structure of 83, 95

mainstream 9, 96, 110, 113,
115-7

science of xvi, 7, 9, 10, 11, 81-2,
110, 118, 143, 155-7

Hume, David 96
humours, theory of 47-8, 49, 53

I

iceberg theory 73
incommensurability 17-21, 90, 116
individualism 87, 127
institutional school 113-8
interest rates 161-2, 163-4, 166, 171
invisible hand 86
isostasy 73, 74

J

James II (King) 146
jigsaw puzzle 41, 70, 72-3, 74, 116,
179
John Paul II (Pope) 43

K

Kelvin, Lord 74
Kepler, Johannes 41-2
Keynes, John Maynard 3, 84, 102
Keynesian
school 102-3, 118
stimulus 165-6, 187-8, 191
kingdoms 144-5
Kirk, Captain 21, 22
Krugman, Paul 7-8
Kuhn, Thomas 10, 17-25, 37, 39,
121

L

Laffer curve 159-60
land-bridge theory 71

Lazear, Edward 81
Lenin 107
Leucippus 33
libertarian school 91, 92
 vs Darwinism 134-8
Life of Brian 89
Luddite movement 108
lump of labour fallacy 107-8
luxury goods 130-1
Lyell, Sir Charles 60

M

macroeconomics 6, 98, 99, 103, 160,
186
Malthus, Robert 63, 125
Malthusian population rates 136-7
Marx, Karl 3, 107
Marxist school 106-11, 118
 vs Darwinism 133-4
maximisation 87, 93, 111-2, 126-7,
129
mechanisation 106
Menanius 55
Minsky
Hyman 103-4
moment 119, 162
Minsky's school 103-5, 118
monetarist school 93-102, 118
monetary
arteries 162
policy 5-6, 11, 163
stimulus 101, 163, 165-6, 180,
187

monopolistic practice 109

Murray, Charles 20

N

natural selection 63-4

neoclassical competitor 126

neoclassical school 25, 81, 84-8, 92, 96, 118

    see also 'equilibrium'

    vs Darwinism 133

Newton, Isaac 42

Newtonian 85, 87, 120

Nietzsche, Friedrich 101

O

Of Money 96

Of Seditions And Troubles 193

oligopolistic practice 109

Omphalos 61

On the Fabric of the Human Body 49

On the Motion of the Heart and Blood 47

On the Origin of Species 59, 61, 64

On the Revolutions of Heavenly Spheres 38

optimisers 113, 128, 129, 131-2, 139

Oreskes, Naomi 71

Owen, Dr Orville W. 55

Owen, Richard 64-6

P

Padua 29, 47, 49, 51

paradigm shift 11, 22-5, 41, 76, 82, 121

paradox of

    gluttony 104

    thrift 102

payday lenders 161

policymakers 3-4, 8, 9, 100, 157, 164

Primrose, James 53

private sector 5-6, 86, 94, 103, 137, 158, 160-1

productivity arms race 106-7, 108

Ptolemaic model 34, 36-7, 44

Ptolemy 34-7

Q

quantitative easing (QE) 7, 11, 102, 164-5, 180, 186-8

R

redeployment 108

Reid, Harry Fielding 74-5

Rejection of Continental Drift, The 71

Rise and Fall of Monetarism, The 100

retrograde motion 33-5

S

Saboteur movement 108

Saez, Emmanuel 109-10

secular stagnation 180

self-interest 85-6, 92-3, 115, 138

Shakespeare, William 54-6

Shiller, Robert 10

shrivelling apple model 71

Smith, Adam 3, 63, 84-6, 109, 125, 136

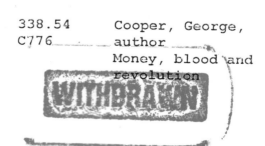